LITERATURE AND TOLERANCE

Views

from Prague

READERS INTERNATIONAL
(PRAGUE)
CZECH CENTER
OF INTERNATIONAL P.E.N.

Readers International (Prague) and the Czech Centre
of International P.E.N. would like to thank
the Ministry of Foreign Affairs of the Czech Republic
and the Ministry of Culture of the Czech Republic,
without whose financial support this book
could never have been published.

LITERATURE AND TOLERANCE: Views from Prague
Translated from the Czech original:
Čeští spisovatelé O TOLERANCI
Cover design: Jan Brychta
First English edition 1994
Published by Readers International (Prague),
in cooperation with the Czech Center of International P.E.N.
Valdštejnské nám. 4
118 00 Praha 1
Czech Republic
Typesetting by Michal Uhde
Printed by Signet spol. s r. o.
Czech Republic

ISBN 0-930523-63-6

Foreword

The last World Congress of International P.E.N. that took place in this city and in this country (which at that time had different borders) was in 1938, shortly before the death of Karel Čapek, *spiritus agens* of that congress, founder and first president of the Czech Center of P.E.N.

My purpose in stating these dry facts is not to anticipate the history of our center, which receives extensive coverage in this book, but merely to remind readers that the foundations Čapek laid some six decades ago remain unshaken, even in the wake of the cruel times our country has seen since. And that Čapek's humanism and ideals, the same as those incorporated in the founding articles of the P.E.N. Charter, are still alive and meaningful, fully two generations later.

For this reason we feel confident that the theme of this congress, „Literature and Tolerance," is just just as important to us here today as it was to Čapek and to all that he strove for in his day. Perhaps it is also because members of the literary community in this country have traditionally served as political figures whenever lawlessness has reared its head. Before as well as after Čapek.

Our view of tolerance has never been a detached one; it has never been based on general interpretations, but has always been honed by historical memory and personal experience. We have always been aware that, unlike justice, tolerance cannot and must not be blind. That is also why we have assembled in this publication a variety of views on the relationship between literature and tolerance. And even if this collection should serve as nothing more than a contemplation of our own tolerance and that of those around us, it will have fulfilled its mission.

To all who peer into the pages that follow, I wish an enjoyable experience both with this book and with the people and places that gave rise to it.

JIŘÍ STRÁNSKÝ
President, Czech Center of International P.E.N.
Prague

Karel Čapek

MAKE ROOM FOR JONATHAN!

*Notes and comments
on public life,
1921-1937*

This Jonathan of mine has not come looking for an office job – it was in a poem of Walt Whitman's that I met him, shouting as he shouldered his way through the crowd to get a good look. "Clear the way!" Here's a man who wants to see what's going on out there. Isn't that what he's here for? To use his eyes, to be in on things and then to "pass the word back to Virginia"? I beg you to take Jonathan's democratic outcry seriously (and indeed to spare a thought for good old Walt Whitman – he deserves it).

You must bear with me. We had been talking about culture and such matters, with solemn faces and warning fingers wagging. We saw culture as a serious commitment and a mission, setting a high standard of appreciation, a hierarchy of excellence, a monasticism of the intellect, a noble and exclusive calling – but also as a service to the community. Now I would not retract a word of all that – I just want to add something that's missing. I would call that an aristocratic idea of culture, one which has its justification, but which does not give the whole picture. It is true that this high-minded culture lands one in a sort of spiritual isolation with its stern and lofty goals; but it is no less true that it liberates one. And what's all this about monasticism? Culture lets you see more and live in a wider world; your gaze is freer and your mind less shackled. You have more varied relationships with other people, more interests to follow up, more attentive wits, more ways of discovering things and taking action. And if that in itself is not a satisfying and endless source of delight, God help you.

If culture is not as enticing, boundless and vital as life itself, we shall glorify it in vain. Nothing is as deadly to culture as the rule of pedants and stuffed shirts, cranky specialists, intellectu-

al "touch-me-nots" and official sponsors, narrow-minded doctri-
naires and dogmatists, learned asses, soured apostles, radical
nit-pickers, neurasthenic aesthetes and egocentrics and the
whole intolerant, narrow-minded, conceited, dry-as-dust and
intolerably boring intellectual élite. A culture that is not liberat-
ing and does not lead to a broader and freer view of the world is
no longer a living culture. If it limits and narrows down the
human mind, it is trapped in a cul-de-sac of its own making.

This is the moment to talk about pride, the cultural hubris we
have just mentioned. There is far too much of it about – look how
often the cultural world pronounces a sentence of annihilating
rejection. How old-fashioned ideas, other people's views, or
those of the habitués of a different literary café, are arrogantly
dismissed out of hand. There is no need to prove anything, all
you have to do is shout loud enough. This is variously called literary criticism, ideological struggle, a matter of principle, or the
generation gap. In truth it is merely prickly intellectual exclu-
siveness running around looking for something to turn up its
nose at. If your nose is in the air, though, you cannot see properly. For my part, I think we were given noses to poke them into
things and not to express our disdain. When you meet someone
with his cultural nose in the air, emitting cries of disgust and
rejection, you can be sure he has nothing of interest to impart.
But since in this vale of tears to hear only too often means to
believe, alas, many will readily be convinced that Peter and Paul
are ignorant fools and swindlers, sick in mind and weak in character, because they have a different opinion on some matter or
other, or because what they do is not what the speaker does. Or
that facts and events which do not fit in with his own beliefs and
sympathies are therefore irrelevant, reprehensible and unwor-
thy of consideration.

Let everyone who disagrees with me be the object of public
scorn: that seems to be the basic principle of our "cultural life" –
as of political journalism. Is there some profound affinity between the two? Nowhere in real life will you find such fierce
contempt and rejection as flourishes in these two paper fields. I

have tried to define the intellectual as one who knows more than
other people and is willing to find out still more. Alas, that is the
ideal intellectual. The real-life one is only too often a man who
condemns and *excludes* more vehemently than other people.

I have described this typical intellectual attitude because it is
just about the opposite of what could be called a broad intellectual horizon, an unprejudiced mind, a liberal spirit, inner freedom, or whatever words fit the moral and spiritual characteristics of one who has no intention of going through life wearing
blinkers. How dull and circumscribed is the world of those who
acknowledge only a few things and reject all the rest! Shackled
by their own way of thinking, they passionately refuse others
the freedom to be different, to think differently, or to work in a
different way. At this point warning eyebrows may be raised,
and mutterings about liberalism no longer working may be
heard. Perhaps it is true that political liberalism has had its day,
but does this mean that freedom, too, has had its day, and if so,
what is going to take its place? I think there is no one among us
in the intellectual professions who would fail to protest loud and
long if anything were to threaten (or has already threatened?)
our right to think and proclaim what we like. Yet strangely
enough, we do not see it as impeding others' freedom if we condemn all and sundry who do not see eye to eye with us, and do
so with the utmost scorn and disdain. Every Tom, Dick and
Harry thinks he has the right to bar others from the society of
the sensible and right-thinking simply because they live by other criteria, do not share his experiences and enjoy other interests. Are you a Marxist or a ruddy bourgeois, do you swear by
Nature in the raw or by sleek urbanism, are you a pure Romantic or an earthbound realist, an individualist or bound to the
collective will? Any one of these labels can bring down cultural
anathema on your head, and then you will be driven from the
community of the elect in shame and derision. There is no room
here for Jonathans who want to get their own angle on the
world. I do not know what to call a society that so eagerly, so
triumphantly and so often rejects and excludes "the other," but
in no way can it be called democratic.

I know, I know... we are men and women of principle. If you are a vegetarian, you don't eat meat on principle, or because you suffer from a poor digestion. Yet you must agree that this is a long way from declaring that Dostoyevsky, say, was a miserable scribbler because he ate meat, or preaching that innoculation against rabies is a foul heresy because as far as we know, Pasteur was not a vegetarian. I am sure we would find such views abysmally stupid, just as we find it stupid and uncouth that so many excellent poets, artists and scholars in Germany today are no longer any good because they are Jewish or because they have their own opinion on certain subjects. Here we are in no doubt that *this* sort of condemnation or assessment has nothing to do with culture. We must be wary, though, and look carefully at some of the cultural judgment passed in our own country. Is it not the case that our cultural values are assessed, accepted or rejected, praised or decried, according to political criteria, from the different standpoints of two generations, by what the times are calling for, by all sorts of vague standards? Not to speak of more personal motives.

Principles, opinions, values... what abstractions! In real life, principles cannot be acquired like books, or a vase, to be taken home and placed on a shelf. It is true that many people do collect their spiritual baggage in this easy fashion, but what we are talking about is the truly spiritual life, not a makeshift substitute. In real life, indeed, opinions, principles, creeds and beliefs grow out of personal experience and real encounters. Views and principles reflect the complete personality, the whole of a man's life and the whole world he has experience of. Some people are romantics, because the fantastic, lovely and terrible romance of life and of the world does in fact exist. Some are realists, because gross, ugly, dirty, everyday reality also exists. This is not to claim that everyone has his own truth, but that every reality is true to life. Beware lest in rejecting opinions we reject reality; beware lest we toss the true living baby out with the intellectual bathwater.

We must never murder reality! Reality is there for us to observe and get to know, to change and revolutionize, but not for us to pick and choose the bits that suit us, to limit, falsify or reject. No one has the whole of reality in his grasp, no one has ever known it in its entirety; it is the common property of all who have ever walked the earth. It is the height of intellectual conceit to assume that what we do not have in our own heads, what we do not know or do not believe, what does not interest us, is null and void and should be contemptuously cast aside. The more limited the mentality, the more conceited the creature, for there is so much more that he does not know and therefore rejects; he is content with one narrow strip of reality, delimited by his own interests and opinions. It is no tragedy that he cannot see beyond the end of his own nose, but it is something of a tragedy if he declares there is nothing there to see, or that whatever it may be, it is worthless and insignificant.

In the real world there are no opinions, but people who opine; if we reject their opinions we are rejecting the people themselves, and it seems to me the height of impertinence to spurn the whole of a man's life. It's a simple matter to reject an opinion – all you need is a sharp tongue and a wave of the hand, but it is far more difficult to convince a man. It means getting him to experience for himself things he has never known and relationships he has never encountered. To convince him of something we have to make it a part of his life.

I am thinking of poets and philosophers, reformers and founders of creeds; these were always men who opened up new fields of experience, gave access to wider knowledge, and unveiled unknown affinities. There is only one way to live a creative life: to change the given state of affairs by adding something desirable that can be absorbed into personal experience. Reality does not exist on one side, with ideals, goals, values and principles somewhere on the other; unless ideals and values are personally experienced and realized as part of ourselves, they are worthless, mere lies, a mockery and a makeshift for real life. The creative spirit comes not to destroy but to fulfill the law; not to reject reality but to change it by adding something new and original. A spirit that reject is the contrary of the spirit that creates.

The trouble is, the spirit that rejects usually believes that it is fighting for something. Let us not take the word "fighting" too literally; real wars and real fights, as is well known, are not won by disregarding the enemy, declaring him a fool and a good-for-nothing whose existence can be ignored. Such people would not be warriors in real conflict; at most they might be dogsbodies sent to make mischief at the enemy's home base. That, too, may play a part in war games, but let us not label it an ideological struggle, heroic defense of principles, a cultural campaign, or what-have-you. It is malingering, and let us put it honestly where it belongs: in political journalism.

In the cultural sphere, though: Make room for Jonathan! Make room for all who offer their experience and their knowledge, their piece of reality. Make room for every vision and every insight! Culture is something shared by all; it is democratic, supremely corporate. Indeed it is the only thing in the whole of the universe that is absolutely common to all; it is general and universal, for its goal is to embrace all reality. It is the only thing that is boundless, for there is no final point at which it stops; it is the only thing that never grows old, for it never ceases to be creative. Take away but one thread from the web of culture, and you have deformed it. Everything that gives expression to any aspect of reality is a part of culture; it suffers only when limitations are imposed on it.

Culture is boundless, and yet you bicker small-mindedly over your place in it. What a cramped and *petty* thing you have made of the intellectual universe!

KAREL ČAPEK (1890–1938)
Dramatist and novelist,
first president
of the Czech P.E.N. Club

Václav Havel

"ON HATRED"

*From an Address
Given in Oslo, Norway,
August 28, 1990*

When I think about the people who have hated me personally, or still do, I realize that they share several characteristics which – when you put them together and analyze them – suggest a certain general interpretation of the origin of their hatred.

They are never hollow, empty, passive, indifferent, apathetic people. Their hatred always seems to me the expression of a large and unquenchable longing, a permanently unfulfilled and unfulfillable desire, a kind of desperate ambition. In other words, it's an active inner capacity that is always leading the person to fixate on something, always pushing him in a certain direction, and is in a sense stronger than he is. I certainly don't think hatred is the mere absence of love or humanity, a mere vacuum in the human spirit. On the contrary, it has a lot in common with love, chiefly with that self-transcending aspect of love, the fixation on others, the dependence on them, and in fact, the delegation of a piece of one's own identity to them. Just as a lover longs for the loved one and cannot get along without him, the hater longs for the object of that hatred. And like love, hatred is ultimately an expression of longing for the absolute, albeit an expression that has become tragically inverted.

People who hate, at least those I have known, harbor a permanent, irradicable feeling of injury, a feeling that is, of course, out of all proportion to reality. It's as though these people wanted to be endlessly honored, loved and respected, as though they suffered from the chronic and painful awareness that others are ungrateful and unforgiveably unjust towards them, not only because they don't honor and love them boundlessly, as they ought, but because they even – or so it seems – ignore them.

In the subconsciousness of the haters there slumbers a perverse feeling that they alone are the true possessors of truth, that they are some kind of superhumans or even gods, and thus

deserve the world's complete recognition, even its complete sub-
missiveness and loyalty, if not its blind obedience. They want to
be the center of the world and are constantly frustrated and ir-
ritated because the world does not accept and recognize them as
such; indeed, it may not even pay any attention to them, and
perhaps it even ridicules them.

They are like spoiled or badly brought up children who think
their mother exists only to worship them, and who think ill of
her because she occasionally does something else, like spend
time with her other children, her husband, a book or her work.
They feel all this as an injustice, an injury, a personal attack, a
questioning of their own sense of self-worth. The inner charge of
energy, which might have been love, is perverted into hatred
towards the imputed source of injury.

In hatred – just as in unhappy love – there is present a desperate kind of transcendentalism: people who hate wish to attain the unattainable and are consumed by the impossibility of
attaining it. They see the cause of this in the shameful world
that prevents them from attaining their object. Hatred is a dia-
bolical attribute of the fallen angel: it is a state of the spirit that
aspires to be God, that may even think it is God, and is torment-
ed by indications that it is not and cannot be. It is the attribute
of a creature who is jealous of God and eats his heart out because the road to the throne of God, where he thinks he should
be sitting, is blocked by an unjust world that is conspiring
against him.

The person who hates is never able to see the cause of his
metaphysical failure in himself and the way he so completely
overestimates his own worth. In his eyes, it is the surrounding
world that is to blame. The problem is that such an offender is
too abstract, vague and incomprehensible. It has to be personified because hatred – as a very particular kind of tumescence of
the soul – requires a particular object. And so the person who
hates seeks out a particular offender. Of course this offender is
merely a stand-in, arbitrarily chosen and therefore easily interchangeable. I have noticed that for the hater, hatred is more
important than its object; he can rapidly change objects without
changing anything essential in the relationship. This is under-

standable: he does not harbor hatred towards a particular person, but to what that person represents: a complex of obstacles to the absolute, to absolute recognition, absolute power, total identification with God, truth and the order of the world. Hatred for one's neighbor, therefore, would seem to be only a physiological embodiment of hatred for the universe that is perceived to be the cause of one's own universal failure.

It is said that those who hate suffer from an inferiority complex. This may not be the most precise way to put it. I would rather say that they are people with a complex based on the fatal perception that the world does not appreciate their true worth.

Another observation seems worth making here: the man who hates does not smile, he merely smirks; he is incapable of making a joke, only of bitter ridicule; he can't be genuinely ironic because he can't be ironic about himself. Only those who can laugh at themselves can laugh authentically. Typical of one who hates is a serious face, quickness to take offense, strong language, shouting, the inability to step outside himself and see his own foolishness.

These qualities reveal someting very significant: the hater utterly lacks a sense of belonging, of taste, shame, objectivity; he lacks the capacity to doubt and ask questions, the awareness of his own transience and in fact the feeling of the transience of all things. All the more, the one who hates does not know the experience of genuine absurdity, that is, the absurdity of his own existence, the feeling of his own alienation, his awkwardness, his failure, his limitations or his guilt. The common denominator of all this is clearly a tragic, almost metaphysical lack of a sense of proportion. The hateful person has not grasped the measure of things, the measure of his own possibilities, the measure of his rights, the measure of his own existence and the measure of recognition and love that he can expect. He wants the world to belong to him with no strings attached; that is, he wants the world's recognition to be limitless. He does not understand that the right to the miracle of his own existence and the recognition of that miracle is something he must earn through his actions. He sees them, on the contrary, as a right granted to him once and for all, unlimited and never called into question. In short, he believes that he has something like an unconditional free pass anywhere, even to heaven. Anyone who dares to scrutinize his pass is an enemy who does him wrong. If this is how he understands his right to existence and recognition, then he must be constantly angry at someone for not drawing the proper conclusions.

I have noticed that all haters accuse their neighbors – and through them the whole world – of being evil. The motive force behind this wrath is the feeling that these evil people and the evil world are denying them what is naturally theirs. In other words, haters project their own anger onto others. Here too they are like spoiled children: they don't see that they must sometimes show themselves worthy of something and that if they don't automatically have everything they think they should, this is not because someone is being nasty to them.

In hatred there is great egocentrism and great self-love. Longing for absolute self-confirmation and not encountering it, hating people feel that they are the victims of an insidious evil, an omnipresent injustice that has to be got to be eliminated to give justice its due. But in their minds, justice is turned on its head. They see it as a duty to grant them something that cannot be granted: the whole world.

The person who hates is unhappy, because whatever he does to achieve full recognition, and to destroy those he thinks are responsible for his lack of recognition, he can never attain the success he longs for, that is, the success of the absolute. Always, from some quarter – for example from the serene, tolerant and forgiving smile of his victim – the full horror of his powerlessness, or rather his incapacity to be God, will be borne in upon him.

Hatred is indivisible; that is, there is no difference between individual hatred and group hatred. Anyone who hates an individual is almost always capable of succumbing to group hatred or even of spreading it. I would even say that group hatred – be it religious, ideological or doctrinal, social, national or any other kind – is a kind of funnel that ultimately draws into itself everyone disposed towards individual hatred. In other words: the most proper background and human potential of all group hatred is a collection of people who are capable of hating individuals.

But more that that: collective hatred shared, spread and deepened by people capable of hatred, has a special magnetic attraction and therefore has the power to draw countless other people into its funnel, people who, though they seem to lack the talent of hatred, are morally weak and selfish people, with lazy intellects, incapable of thinking for themselves and therefore susceptible to the suggestive influence of those who hate.

The attraction of collective hatred – infinitely more dangerous than the hatred of individuals for other individuals – derives from several apparent advantages:

1) Collective hatred eliminates loneliness, weakness, powerlessness, the sense of being ignored or abandoned. This, of course, helps people deal with lack of recognition, of failure, because it offers them a sense of belonging. It creates a strange brotherhood, founded on a simple form of mutual understanding that makes no demands whatsoever: the conditions of membership are easily met, and no one need fear that he will not pass muster. What could be simpler then sharing a common object of aversion and accepting a common "ideology of injury" which justifies the aversion expressed to that object? To say, for instance, that Jews, Gypsies, Germans, Arabs, Blacks, Vietnamese, Hungarians or Czechs are responsible for all the misery of the world, and above all for the despair in every wronged soul, is so easy and so understandable! You can always find enough Vietnamese, Hungarians, Czechs, Gypsies or Jews whose behavior can be made to illustrate the idea that they are responsible for everything.

2) The community of those who hate offers another great advantage to its members: they can endlessly reassure each other of their worth, either through exaggerated expressions of hatred for the chosen group of offenders, or through a cult of symbols and rituals that affirms the worth of the hating community. Uniforms, common dress, insignia, flags and favorite songs

bring the participants closer together, confirm their identity, increase, strengthen and multiply their value in their own eyes.

3) Whereas individual aggressiveness is always risky because it raises the specter of individual responsibility, a society of hating individuals in a sense "legalizes" aggressiveness. Expressing it as a group creates the illusion of legitimacy or at least the sense of a "common cover." Hidden within a group, a pack or a mob, every potentially violent person can dare to do more; each one eggs the other on, and all of them – precisely because there are more of them – justify one another.

4) Ultimately the principle of group hatred considerably simplifies the lives of all those who hate and all those who are incapable of independent thinking, because it offers them a very simple and, almost at first sight or first hearing, a recognizable object of hatred: the process of manifesting the general injustice of the world in a particular person who therefore must be hated, is made wonderfully easier if the "offender" is immediately identifiable by the color of his skin, his name, his language, his religion or his place of residence on the globe.

Collective hatred has another insidious advantage: the modest circumstances of its birth. There are many common and seemingly innocent states of mind that create the almost unnoticeable antecedents to potential hatred, a wide and fertile field on which the seeds of hatred will quickly germinate and take root.

Let me give you three examples:

Where can this feeling of universal injustice flourish better than where genuine injustice has been done? Feelings of not being appreciated, logically enough, grow best in a situation where someone has been humiliated, insulted or cheated. The best environment for a chronic feeling of injury is one in which genuine injury is being done. In short, collective hatred gains its veracity and allure most easily wherever a group of people lives in genuine want, that is, in an environment of human misery.

A second example: the miracle of human thought and human reason is bound up with the capacity to generalize. It is hard to imagine the history of the human spirit without this great pow-

er. In a sense, anyone who thinks generalizes. On the other
hand, the ability to generalize is a very fragile gift that has to be
handled with great care. A less perceptive soul can very easily
overlook the hidden seeds of injustice that may lie in the act of
generalization. We have all made observations or expressed
opinions of one kind or another about various peoples: we may
say that the French, the English or the Russians are like this or
like that; we don't mean ill by it, we are only trying, through our
generalizations, to see reality better. But there is a grave danger
hidden in precisely this kind of generalization: that a group of
people defined in a certain way – in this case ethically – is, in a
sense, subtly deprived of individual spirits and individual re-
sponsibilities, and we endow it with an abstract, collective sense
of responsibility. Clearly, this is a wonderful starting point for
collective hatred: individuals become *a priori* bad or evil simply
because of their origin. The evil of racism, one of the worst evils
in the world today, depends among other things directly on this
type of careless generalization.

Finally, the third antecedent of collective hatred I wish to
mention here is something I would call collective "otherness."
One aspect of the immense and wonderful color and mystery of
life is not only that each person is different and that no one can
perfectly understand anyone else, but also that groups of people
differ from each other as groups: in their customs, their traditions, their temperament, their way of life and thinking, their
hierarchy of values, and of course in their faith, the color of their
skin and their way of dressing and so on. This "otherness" is
truly collective and it's quite understandable that the "otherness" of one group can make it seem, to the group we belong to,
surprising, alien and even ridiculous. And just as we are surprised at how different others are, so others are surprised by us
and how different we are from them.

This "otherness" of different communities can of course be
accepted with understanding and tolerance as something that
enriches life; it can be honored and respected, it can even be
enjoyed. But by the same token, it can also be a source of misunderstanding and aversion towards others. And therefore – once
again – it is a fertile ground for future hatred.

Few of those who move on the thin, ambiguous and dangerous terrain created by the awareness of genuine wrong, the ability to generalize and the awarness of "otherness," can from the outset detect the presence of the cuckoo's eggs of collective hatred that can be laid in this terrain, or which have already been laid there.

Some observers today have described Central and Eastern Europe as a powder keg, an area of growing nationalism, ethnic intolerance and expressions of collective hatred. This area is even often described as a possible source of future European instability and of serious threat to peace. In the subtext of such pessimistic reflections, one can sense, here and there, a kind of nostalgia for the good old days of the Cold War, when the two halves of Europe kept each other in check and thanks to which there was peace.

I don't share the pessimism of such observers. Even so, I admit that the corner of the world from which I come could become – even if we did not maintain vigilance and common sense – favorable soil in which collective hatred could grow. This is so for many more or less understandable reasons.

In the first place, you have to realize that in Central and Eastern Europe live many nations and ethnic groups that have blended together in various ways. It is almost impossible to imagine an ideal border that would separate these nations and ethnic groups into territories of their own. Thus there are many minorities, and minorities within minorities, and the existing borders are sometimes rather artificial, so that in fact it's a kind of international melting pot. At the same time, these nations have had very few historic opportunities to seek their own political identity and their own statehood. For centuries, they lived under the shelter of the Austro-Hungarian monarchy and after a brief pause between the wars they were, in one way or another, subjugated by Hitler and then immediately, or shortly thereafter, by Stalin. The nations of Western Europe had decades and centuries to develop to where they are; Central European nations had only twenty years between the two world wars.

Understandably, then, they carry within their collective unconsciousness a feeling that history has done them wrong. An exaggerated feeling of injustice, one precondition of hatred, could quite logically find the right setting for its development here.

The totalitarian system which held sway in most of these countries for so long, was outstanding, among other things, for its tendency to make everything the same, to control and coordinate things, to make them uniform. For decades, it harshly suppressed whatever authenticity – or, if you like, "otherness" – the subject nations had. From the structure of the state administration to the red stars on the rooftops, everything was the same, that is, imported from the Soviet Union. Is it surprising, then, that the moment these countries rid themselves of the totalitarian system, they suddenly perceived, with unusual clarity, their mutual and suddenly liberated "otherness"? And would it be any wonder if this long invisible and therefore necessarily untested and intellectually undigested "otherness" did not cause surprise? Rid of the uniforms and masks that were imposed on us, we are looking for the first time into each others' real faces. Something has come about that might be called the "shock of otherness." And this has given rise to another favorable condition for collective aversion, which in the right circumstances could grow into collective hatred.

The simple fact is that not only have the nations of this area not had enough time to mature as states, they have not had enough time to get used to each other's politically defined otherness.

Here we may once more invoke a comparison with children: in many regards these nations have simply not had enough time to became political adults.

After all they have gone through, they feel a natural need to make their existence quickly visible and to achieve recognition and acknowledgment. They simply wish to be known, to be consulted along with the rest of the world. They want their special "otherness" to be acknowledged. And at the same time, still full of inner uncertainty about themselves and the degree of recognition they enjoy, they look at each other somewhat nervously and ask each other whether those other nations – who moreover have suddenly become as different as they themselves – are not stealing some of the attention that is rightfully theirs.

For years the totalitarian system in this part of Europe suppressed civic autonomy and the rights of individuals, whom it tried to turn into pliant cogs in its machine. This lack of civic culture, which the system destroyed over so many years, and the demoralizing pressure of that system, can in the end create the right conditions for the careless generalizing that always goes along with national intolerance. Respect for human rights, which rejects the principle of collective responsibility, derives from a minimum level of civic culture.

It may be clear from this rather brief and necessarily simplified account that in our part of Europe, conditions are relatively favorable for the rise of national intolerance or even hatred.

There is one more important factor here: after the initial joy at our own liberation comes the inevitable phase of disappointment and depression. It is only now, when we can describe and name everything truthfully, that we see the full extent of the awful legacy left to us by the totalitarian system, and we realize how long and difficult will be the task of repairing all the damage.

This state of general frustration may provoke some to vent their anger on substitute victims, who will stand as proxies for the main and now liquidated offender, the totalitarian system. Helpless rage seeks its own lightning rod.

I repeat that if I speak of the dangers of nationalistic hatred in Central and Eastern Europe, I'm not talking about it as our certain future, but as a potential threat.

We must understand this threat in order to confront it effectively. It is a task that faces all of us who live in the former Soviet bloc.

We must struggle energetically against all the incipient forms of collective hatred, not only on the principle that evil must always be confronted, but also in our own interest.

The Hindus have a legend concerning a mythical bird called Bherunda. The bird has a single body, but two necks, two heads and two separate consciousnesses. After an eternity together, these two heads begin to hate each other and decide to do harm to each other. Both of them swallow pebbles and poison and the result is predictable: the whole Bherunda bird goes into spasms and dies with loud cries of pain. It is brought back to life by the infinite mercy of Krishna, to remind people that all hatred harms not only the object of that hatred, but at the same time, and perhaps chiefly, the one who hates.

We who live in the newly created democracies of Europe should remind ourselves of this legend each day: as soon as one of us succumbs to the temptation to hate another, we will all end up like the Bherunda bird.

With this difference: there will be no earthly Krishna on hand to liberate us from our new misfortune.

VÁCLAV HAVEL (1936)
Dramatist and essayist
Prague

Lumír
Čivrný

GOOD
AND BAD TIMES
Seventy Years
of the Czech PEN Club

If we think of history as a vast and boundless river surging relentlessly onwards, it is tempting to imagine this Amazon rolling over and obliterating any event as if it had never been; and indeed the event is no more. The trouble is that we cannot say what the river of history would be like if in fact nothing had happened; that something did indeed happen precludes any alternative. Yet at the same time this makes it difficult, if not impossible, to determine what the effect of that happening really was, precisely because history is all-embracing in its vastness. It encompasses all things, even that which never was, just as non-existence, by its very nature, enfolds being.

It could perhaps be said that the Czech PEN Club was founded in Prague in 1925 in consequence of the inconsistency of Karel Čapek and the consistent perseverance of the English PEN Club.

In his "Letters from England," Čapek expressed some doubt as to whether clubs could exist in his homeland: "Our tradition does not rest on such old and comfortable armchairs; because it has nothing to sit on, it remains hanging in the air." That was in the chapter on clubs, but he confessed to even graver doubts when he wrote, "The Continental talks to show his importance, the Englishman keeps quiet," and went on, "His silence is not that of the solitary, nor of a Pythagorean philosopher; it is not silence before God, nor the silence of death, nor mute, profound meditation; it is unique, a refined social phenomenon, the silence of a gentleman among gentlemen."

Now that our Club is seventy years old, seventy years of meetings, general assemblies, lectures, congresses, conferences and all sorts of talk, it gives one gooseflesh to read what Čapek said of English clubs: "Nobody says a word, which is truly most dignified. We, too, need a place where people don't talk."

In fact we had such a place, all the years the PEN Club was prohibited, but for the rest – it cannot be denied that we talked. As a sign of repentance, or awareness, perhaps we could introduce days, or at least hours, when nobody would speak in our PEN Club.

To come back to the birth of the Club, which is a story in itself: when Mrs. Dawson-Scott thought of founding our PEN Club, she saw it as a way of building up international understanding and peace through the work of writers, those creators of public opinion. So we are told by Professor Otakar Vočadlo in his book, *Karel Čapek's Letters from England*. For many years her house had served as the organizational center for the London PEN Club, founded there on October 5, 1921.

Mrs. Dawson-Scott's daughter Marjorie had already enlisted Professor Vočadlo's help in the autumn of 1922, and since he then lived in London, as a member of the international committee, he was given the task of persuading Czech writers to set up a PEN center in Prague. However, as he writes, he did not meet with understanding, and so towards the end of the year he appealed to Karel Čapek for help, with a detailed account of the aims and significance of the PEN Club. Čapek's answer was to "... put the matter of the PEN Club to the Syndicate of Czech Writers, who should create a center to be affiliated with the PEN Club."

It appears to be part of our democratic tradition to pass the buck, and we need not complain if it still lives on.

However, the English did not like this idea of a Syndicate half-breed, preferring a thoroughbred PEN Club. Čapek had to find someone else to take the job on. This was František Khol, engineer and writer active in the theater, who took the matter in hand, so to speak, and wrote to Vočadlo on February 14, 1924, that the "Prague branch of the PEN Club had been set up." However, it had not been set up firmly enough to survive, although Khol was no mean hand at passing the buck: "Everything is in order, and if anyone comes we'll let Hanuš Jelínek look after him, because he has enough time to spare."

As thus established, the PEN Club had a chairman, honorary secretary, honorary treasurer and a committee consisting of Jelínek, Khol, Kosterka, Čapek, Dyk, Jež, Křička, Medek, Opolský, Sezima, Skácelík and Vočadlo, but seemed to lack balance or bond, for on November 8, 1924, Khol again wrote to Vočadlo in London, telling him that "we are getting the PEN Club together again and this time it'll really be serious."

Getting something together again when it had already been set up once suggests that the Club was not so serious after all. But now Čapek had taken things in hand: "Čapek and I are busy getting things going" – and Čapek clearly felt it was his responsibility; on Christmas Day he invited G. K. Chesterton to come to Prague in the spring as a guest of the newly established PEN Club.

It is not easy to get things going; in the case of a writers' association, if it is not to fall apart at once, it is more like giving birth than founding or establishing. The Czech PEN Club can be said to have been born on February 15, 1925, at eleven in the morning, in the Café Louvre. The birth is registered in the minutes of this meeting, witnessed by all the names on the list of those present.

A few words about the place of birth: the Café Louvre stood, as is well known, about two-thirds of the way along Národní Street (just about where the blows from police batons fell thickest on the demonstrators' heads in November 1989). The Union Café was just opposite, with its famous head waiter Mr. Patera, of blessed memory; he not only waited on his artist customers, but sometimes paid their bills. Today the modern childrens' bookshop Albatros stands on the Union site, while almost next door the Metro Café still remembers its role as the meeting-place of avant-garde intellectuals in the thirties. Further on, Paukert's wine cellar was visited almost daily by Viktor Dyk, while still further in the same direction one came to the Národní Café on the first floor, at that time the property of the family of the poet Jaroslav Kolman-Cassius, and as popular a meeting-place for writers as the more famous Café Slavia on the corner where the street meets the embankment. Between these two cafés stood the Academy of Sciences and the Topič building, home of Borový's publishing house and later the Writers Union with its attendant institutions. Opposite the Café Slavia stands the National Theater, the "golden shrine" of the Czechs, with the Želmíra wine cellar nearby, and beyond the church and a side street, the Réva wine cellar (later to become the cultural center and bookshop of the German Democratic Republic, and in its last incarnation the seat of the British Council). Next came the Café Louvre, Vilímek's bookshop, the Publishing Cooperative with the Folk Arts Center and the Odeon publishing house, and finally the Theater Beyond the Gate, the Laterna Magica and of course Voleský's bookshop. In this somewhat anachronistic list we have probably omitted more than the State Film Lending Library.

Probably nowhere in the world could one find so many buildings devoted to the service of the mind – including those that serve the soul – concentrated in so small a space. Walking down Národní Street, any person of genius could be sure of meeting a kindred spirit, and were the adjective "Národní" – national – not so time-honored, this Prague street could be aptly called Genius Street.

Karel Čapek was thus drawing on the spiritual depths of Národní Street when he chose the Café Louvre as the birthplace of the PEN Club, and the minutes report his speech to the newborn: "Dr. K. Čapek in the chair welcomed all those present and explained the purpose of the PEN Club. This was primarily to encourage personal contacts between Czechoslovak and other writers; he himself had seen the favorable results achieved by the English PEN Club in that respect, when he was in England. Members of the Club would meet once a month and would invite foreign writers to address them. The importance of providing the right milieu for distinguished foreign guests can best be seen from the case of Wells. Up to the present it has been the responsibility of the Ministry of Foreign Affairs to look after such guests, but this has not always been ideal. Our foreign visitors would like to see something of the way we live. The Club will also encourage contacts among Czechoslovak writers themselves, particularly Slovak writers who come to Prague. Financial support from government funds will be available to provide hospitality for foreign guests, and it is therefore important to find suitable premises for the Club. Dr. Čapek then asked those present to propose new members at the next meeting, adding, however, that the committee would discuss every individual proposed for membership. The main tasks of the future committee would be to make arrangements. What the Club would be like depended on what its members did."

Čapek's final words, simple and unemotional, should echo on as an exhortation for the future.

The sixteenth of February, nineteen hundred and twenty-five: our PEN Club is born. Books are written and published, because publishing goes on as usual. Some publishers are obviously "better" than others, and the Modern Publishers Club Kmen was soon to unite those with cultural ambitions: Borový, Topič, Petr, Laichter, Kvasnička and Hampl, Sfinx-Janda, Melantrich, Hudební matice Umělecké besedy. The Publishing Cooperative was founded, in which readers and their publisher cooperated and which later gave birth to ELK books. Bookshops spread all over the Czech and Moravian-Silesian countryside, the people working in them trained by the Booksellers Cooperative, not just shop assistants who would not know what a book was, or what was in it, or even whether they had it on their shelves. The Publishers and Booksellers Union trained their people and saw to it that they behaved accordingly, and published a paper for them. The same was true of Slovakia, and mention of the fact in Bohemia was not yet branded as "interference in internal affairs." The Czechoslovak Republic was still young, but it already awarded state prizes for good books, and among the PEN Club members thus distinguished was the chairman Karel Čapek, for his play *R.U.R.* and the novel *Krakatit*, K. M. Čapek-Chod for his novels *Antonín Vondrejc* and *Vilém Rozkoč*, and Božena Benešová for her novels *Člověk* and *Úder*. The young film industry commissioned screenplays of new books (K. M. Čapek-Chod's *Humoresque*). State prizes were given to those who wrote in German, and there was little political discrimination – the Catholic Jaroslav Durych was as respected as the communist Vladislav Vančura. The plays of František Langer, Jaroslav Hilbert, Edmond Konrád – and of course those of Karel Čapek – were played to full houses, while amateur theater flourished; in

the country, culture was very much alive without the blessing of
central control. The atmosphere needs no description, inspiration flows naturally from one focus to another, one work inspires
another and everything is part of the whole. Young people are
hungry for novelty and first nights, nor do their elders feel out of
the picture. What is to be said can be said without string-pulling
or obsequious flattery. Bold innovations are thrown down like
challenges to society, challenges that are serious. Strata of society, groups and circles that consider culture their lifeblood,
emerge, people for whom to be is more important than to have.
The war and its aftermath have thrown up greedy new rich, not
to mention the new poor, who will become ever more numerous
as the world economic crisis comes closer to this little country,
which is trying to make up for centuries of foreign oppression.
Neither in politics nor in culture does this country want to be
isolationist, but these are its first steps on its own. Čapek's PEN
Club, too, goes forward with no insistence on ideology. "It will be
what its members make of it," but what its founders want to
make of the club is clear from the outset.

And who might they be? In the first place, people who can be
depended on in delicate cultural and social situations, people
like Otokar Fischer, Hanuš Jelínek, Vilém Mathesius, and Václav Tille. People who have a good university background, of
course, but more significant is their reputation for talent. They
all speak and write in languages outside their speciality, Fischer
the German scholar, Jelínek the specialist in Romance languages, Mathesius the authority in English. Both Fischer and
Jelínek are poets in their own right as well as translators of
poetry; Mathesius is the future chairman of the Prague Linguistic Circle, which will give birth to structuralism, with Roman Ja-
kobson, Mukařovský and Bogatyrev as midwives. And Václav
Tille? This lecturer on comparative literary studies, whose bold
forays into world literature enchant his students, publishes an
exemplary study of Božena Němcová and a delightful book of
fairy tales under the pseudonym Václav Říha. Each of these literary personalities was constantly in the public eye as a critic,
primarily of the theater. Indeed, it almost looks as though they
were responsible for the remarkable outburst of Czech dramatic

talent between the two world wars. Together, of course, with the
playwrights themselves, František Langer, Edmond Konrád, Jaroslav Kvapil, Fráňa Šrámek. Not to mention Karel Čapek. They
are all founding members of the PEN Club, along with the
women writers Božena Benešová and Anna Maria Tilschová,
both born in 1873 and signal names in the history of the modern
Czech novel from the 1920's onward. Marie Pujmanová, twenty
years their junior, added her talents to theirs.

Of the thirty-eight people present when the PEN Club was
established, the members of the first committee can be thought
to have been fatefully chosen by Karel Čapek. Without Čapek,
the Czech PEN Club would have waited long; as it was, it followed on the heels of the English club. In February 1925 Čapek
was only thirty-five, but he was already well known in the world
for his plays *R. U. R., From the Live of the Insects* and *The Macro-
pulos Affair*, and for his travels in England which led to his determination to found the Czech PEN Club. On this trip he exer-
cised his charm on the best-known English writers of the day,
Galsworthy, Wells, Shaw and Chesterton, a pleasant conversationalist with a delightful sense of humor, capable of making
himslef at home with his intellectual witticisms even in new and
unknown surroundings. Vočadlo has given eloquent testimony to
Čapek's success, and František Langer's words on the tenth anniversary of Čapek's death testify to the versatility of this writer
and journalist, playwright and poet, artist and photographer, ar-
chaeologist versed in the art of indigenous peoples, gardener
and vintager and wine taster as well: "He was delightful in his
cups, when he had just enough to start singing his grandmoth-
er's songs, or to talk endlessly, taking on the whole world and
making his peace even with his enemies. His cheeks were even
more flushed, his eyes gleamed and his boyish mouth pursed
and puckered, the tuft at the back of his head stood on end and
the neat parting disappeared as his hair drooped over his eyes."

Anna Lauermannová, forty-four years older than Čapek, at
seventy-seven was the link between the newly founded PEN
Club and the literary revival of the 19th century, not only because as a small child she had reached up to the doorknobs of the
Palacký and Rieger family homes, but for her own legendary

salon where from 1880 onwards many a literary generation came to take tea. She was the author of a number of novels and stories under the pseudonym Felix Téver. Had she been French she could have written to Voltaire in the words of Madame du Deffand: "It is your spirit that contents me." Here in Bohemia, looking down from the Prague Castle, she wrote: " The Prague of my childhood was the Prague of history, its hundred towers enmeshed in dream of the past, and in its chimes rang the echo of previous generations." She had long been affectionately known as "Granny," and when she died on June 16, 1932, in the PEN Club all remembered her skill at smoothing sharp edges and bridging differences.

Anna Marie Tilschová and Božena Benešová were both fifty-two when the PEN Club was founded, and devoted themselves selflessly to it for many years. Božena Benešová, awarded two state prizes, excelled in portraying the oppressive atmosphere of the time of the first world war. Her subtle insights into feminine psychology captivated even the younger generation when in the year of her death she published *Don Pablo, Don Pedro and Věra Lukášová*, later one of the most popular dramatizations of E. F. Burian's theater. The silence that later blanketed her work was a sin. For eleven years this poetic soul served the PEN Club in the thankless post of treasurer.

In 1934 A. M. Tilschová took over the chairmanship of the Club from Čapek, when after repeated attempts at resignation he finally insisted on giving it up. She guided it well in the difficult days before the war, when the Club flourished in the run-up to the 1938 Congress, and then with the Czechoslovak Republic lived through the occupation of 1939 and on to 1942 when the Gestapo closed the Club down. She guided it through the revival of 1945 and up to its 1948 transmogrification into an organization officially sanctioned by the authorities, when post-February diplomacy replaced her with Marie Majerová. On the eve of her seventy-fifth birthday, November 8, 1948, A. M. Tilschová acquitted herself with fortitude at the evening organized in her honor by six societies: the Artists Club, the PEN Club, the Božena Němcová Society, the Council of Women, the Writers Syndicate and the Artists Society (Beseda), under the aegis of two ministers: Zdeněk Nejedlý and Václav Kopecký. When she died on June 18, 1957, the PEN Club was no longer represented on the death notice; nothing but the Ministry of Education and Culture and the Writers Union. Her monumental novels *An Old Family, Sons* and *Mine Tips* are of great importance in the evolution of Czech psychological and social prose, but neither the novels nor her short stories have been fortunate in new editions.

When the PEN Club was established, Hanuš Jelínek was forty-seven. A lyric poet and translator, literary and dramatic critic, he was an irreplaceable link between Czech and French literature. Over fifty translations from the French cover all the genres: folk poetry, medieval love lyrics, modern French poetry from Baudelaire to Cocteau, classical and modern plays as well as such major prose works as Martin du Gard's *The Thibaults*. His mastery of both tongues was such that he could present Czech literature to the French in such books as *L'histoire de la littérature tchèque*, a volume of *Études tchècoslovaques*, and translations of Karel Čapek (*R.U.R.*), Viktor Dyk (*Morning Toad*) and the Romantic Karel Hynek Mácha's masterpiece, *May*. Son-in-law of Alois Jirásek and friend of Viktor Dyk, František Halas and Jaroslav Seifert, he gazed benevolently at the exuberant young writers of the thirties. Up to his death in 1944, he was a familiar figure with his neat imperial beard and mustache, a gallant and subtle conversationalist whom not even speech difficulties after a throat operation could discountenance. All PEN Club links with the Romance language countries during that time bear the stamp of Jelínek's precise initiatives, vast knowledge and chivalrous nature.

In that he was rivalled by Otokar Fischer, five years his junior. An original poet and playwright, scholar and literary critic, his lectures at the Faculty of Arts enchanted his listeners with portraits of classical and Romantic German writers, rich in magical detail, delivered without notes. His keen mind and his erudition enabled him to penetrate the finest web of writing and the springs of creative genius, while his broad knowledge of the intellectual world allowed him to follow other branches as well, in particular literary psychology, history and criticism. As a translator he gave us the unforgettable Villon and Faust; as a poet, six volumes of verse and as many plays; as a literary critic and historian, monographic studies of Kleist, Nietsche and Heine, F. X. Šalda, the National Theater, literary psychology and criticism; and two excellent volumes of essays, *The Spirit and the Word*, and *The Word and the World*. His dramatic criticism and newspaper columns offered a daily commentary on cultural life, and when Fascism rose to threaten Europe he threw all his authority behind the defense of freedom and democracy. This tireless scholar had too delicate a heart, however, and Hitler's attack on Austria so shocked him that he suffered a fatal heart attack – the first victim of Nazism in Czech culture. Some months before Karel Čapek...

Nor had Václav Tille, another shining light of Charles University, long to serve the PEN Club. He joined the committee in 1929, and died in 1937, like F. X. Šalda.

The infant PEN Club made an active start in life, the committee gathering for its first meeting three days later, in Karel Čapek's apartment in Říční Street in the Little Quarter. The principal business was an invitation to President Masaryk, to honor the Club's first dinner in the Municipal Rooms of the capital. This would be a celebration of his seventy-fifth birthday and of the publication of his memoirs. Ignát Herrmann would preside. One week later, on February 28th, four new members were accepted into the Club: František Götz, Adolf Hoffmeister, Josef Kodíček and Ferdinand Peroutka, all then young men. The committee also agreed to ask the appropriate ministry for a grant of fifteen thousand crowns. The most significant thing, however, was the clear stand taken by the chairman both for the present, and – farsightedly – for the future: that it was essential to invite German writers in Czechoslovakia to join the Club.

Naturally those German writers who were not interested in cooperation would not be approached, but there were others, and a fortnight later the committee agreed to the following ten names: J. Aehrenfels, O. Baum, P. Leppin, H. Salus, R. Thomas, W. Tschuppik, J. Urzidil, J. Weselski and O. Winder. Something was coming into being that not even the generation of 1848 (Kapper, Meisner, Hartmann, Uffo Horn) had dreamed of: reciprocity. On both sides stood writers whose work in either language was legitimately at home in the country. This reciprocity soon bore fruit, and Czech experts in German literature, like Otokar Fischer, were joined by writers like Max Brod and Rudolf Fuchs, who became indefatigable promoters of Czech culture in the broadest sense. Pavel Eisner, polyglot and phenomenal translator, showed his affectionate familiarity with the Czech language in his Balbinesque apologia "Fort and Shrine." Alas, this reciprocity was nipped in the bud almost at once, when Hitler began to strangle our bilingual culture in 1939, a crime which was consummated after 1945 as Stalinism strengthened its hold. Today it is clear that this crippling of Czech culture has been to the detriment of European culture as a whole.

At dinner with President Masaryk, the PEN Club proudly aligned itself behind him, recalling that on his return to the country in 1918 he had stressed the political significance of reciprocity by visiting the German Theater in Prague – and how the self-styled patriots of the day had castigated this policy of mutual respect (and were still to abuse both Masaryk and Karel Čapek and the PEN Club, for not currying favor with the Nazis).

For the time being there was still peace, and in June the Club arranged a third dinner. This time the guest of honor was the French writer M. Rosny, while Marina Tsvetayeva was also present, accompanied by Professor Lyatski of the Faculty of Arts. As so often, to be the guest of the PEN Club could have an influence on one's place in literary history.

In 1926 the chairman was Karel Čapek, the secretary František Khol, with A. M. Tilschová and the historian J. Šusta as vice-chairpersons, B. Benešová as treasurer and J. Tůmová as executive secretary. The other members of the committee were Anna Lauermannová-Mikschová, Marie Pujmannová, V. Červinka, H. Jelínek, O. Fischer and V. Mathesius, with Dohalský and Hoffmeister as deputies. The membership fee was 60 crowns.

Dohalský and Jelínek were sent to attend the International PEN Congress in Berlin, and returned with Mrs. Dawson-Scott, so she could see for herself how the infant Club was getting on. She found it thriving. Indeed, three days later a dinner was given for John Galsworthy, and among the guests were Edmund Husserl and the Croatian poet Gustav Krklec.

To make up for uncertainty about the future visit of G. B. Shaw, G. K. Chesterton and H. G. Wells, E. A. Benett, Hugh Walpole, Frank Swinnerton and John Drinkwater arrived. It was no wonder that the Czech Club was grateful for financial help from the Ministry of Foreign Affairs – and accepted as members Dr. M. Hodža and Dr. J. Preiss.

There were two stars in the sky of October 1926: on the ninth of that month the dinner guest of honor was Rabindranath Tagore, at sixty-four well-known to the Czech public in translation; besides his masterpieces *Gitenjali, Sadhanna* and *The Gardener*, we knew *The King of the Dark Chamber, The Post Office, The Wreck* and the essays on nationalism. The sage's hair and flowing beard were venerably white; dozens of years later his name was brought before the people of Prague again, with a magical exhibition of the drawings and water-colors which he chose as his medium when he gave up writing. A week or two after that memorable dinner, on the state holiday of October 28th (Foundation of the Republic), another Nobel Prize winner honored the Club's table: Paul Valéry, the prince of poets. Seated between Čapek and Jelínek, he was accompanied by Messieurs Dominois, Fichelle, Pasquier and Pauphilet, representing French cultural interests in Prague, and by Dr. Urzidil. The visits of such great men as Tagore and Valéry gave the Czech PEN Club the international standing already enjoyed by the orientalists, of whom the Indologist V. Lesný was also active in the Club, and the Romance scholars.

From the outset contacts between the PEN Club and French writers were prolific. In December Claude Farrere visited, and Franz Werfel was present on that occasion. In May the younger writers Philippe Soupault and Leon Pierre-Quint arrived, followed in November by Benjamin Crémieux, who became a very loyal friend. The Russian poet Konstantin Balmont came from Paris, too; his translations include Czech lyric poetry.

It was clear that the activities of the PEN Club were awakening the slumbering potential of Czech cultural life, and that something new was in the air. "In over a thousand years of unbroken continuity," Professor Vilém Mathesius wrote later, "we have had an undoubted claim to respect for our cultural traditions, but their viability has been made uncertain by dramatic changes in the course of our country's history." The twenty years between the two wars can be seen now as something positive against the background of these dramatic but negative changes, and the work of the PEN Club from 1925 to 1938 was undoubtedly on the positive side, all the more so since it was practical and not just pathetic words. We could have been reacting to other words of Mathesius, in his essay entitled *Opportunities Awaiting Us*, published during the Nazi occupation of the country: "To put into a few words what most hinders us in being good laborers in a good cause, I would say that we lack true humility, that which teaches us to accept what is our true task and to bear patiently the difficulties and failures it brings." The force of these words is enhanced by the fact that they come from so pioneering a scholar as a founder of structural linguistics.

From its inception the Czech Club was open to the whole world, and during the post-Munich years this led to imputations of cosmopolitan snobbery and imitating the fashions of western capitals. In reality the Club was all-embracing, welcoming creative souls of all literary schools and generations.

In June 1927 the Prague PEN Club celebrated the birthdays of Otakar Březina, Jaroslav Kvapil, Jakub Deml, Hanuš Jelínek and P. Leppin, followed by that of Bohdan Kaminský, all of whom except Březina were able to be present. Čapek, Langer and Kvapil joined in greeting the Yugoslav playwright Milan Begović.

Up to 1929, the committee of the Club remained unchanged, except for the co-option of František Langer. Čapek once again offered his resignation because of opposition from right-wing members, but was prevailed upon by Dr. Šusta to remain in office. This was all to the good, for he then worked to recruit young writers – František Götz, Josef Knap, Vítězslav Nezval, A. C. Nor and Vladislav Vančura.

A year later, at the end of January, the Club lost its secretary František Khol, who had been instrumental in its foundation. The author of several books of short stories, Khol also published a biography of Casanova and edited his correspondence. He was also active in the National Theater, but poor health allowed him little over fifty years of life. The playwright Edmond Konrád was co-opted to take Khol's place.

That February Mrs. Dawson-Scott came back to Prague, the foster mother of a worldwide brood of PEN Clubs. We welcomed the Latvian writer Martha Grimma Gusetina, the French novelist and essayist André Thérive and the Polish writer Emil Zegalowicz. The Czech Club was thus open to all sides, while at home it welcomed the composer J. B. Foerster, Arno Kraus and the head of the Writers Syndicate, Karel Scheinpflug.

The committee was reinforced not only by Edmond Konrád but also by the playwright František Langer, a founding member of the Club, and one who with Karel Čapek brought contemporary figures on to the stage at home and abroad. And by Václav Tille, an ally whose contribution has already been mentioned.

At the end of April 1930 the Czech PEN Club welcomed another famous Frenchman, André Maurois, and later in the year two Slav writers, Sophie Nalkowska from Poland and Djuro Dimović from Yugoslavia, who came for the premiere of his play, *Prince Marko*.

It was about this time that the Czech Club applied its diplomatic skills to the sphere of Slovak-Hungarian relations. The Hungarian PEN Club had complained publicly of Czechoslovak censors interfering with their mail sent to the Hungarian minority in Slovakia; the Czech Club sent an official note to the Ministry of the Interior and to the Budapest PEN Club, a tactical move which proved to be wise. When in September of that year three Hungarian writers in Slovakia applied for membership in the Czech PEN Club (Luhász, Lányi and Sándor), our club avoided conflict with the newly formed Slovak PEN Club by sending a delegation to Bratislava: Čapek, Langer and Tille took with them a financial donation to give the new Club a good start.

Guests of the Czech Club in October 1931 included Dora Gabe of Bulgaria and Georges Duhamel. The speech by Otokar Fischer in the latter's honor (on October 26th) has been preserved in the archives, testifying to the high standards of the Club, appreciated during the visit of Luc Durtain by the Minister for

Foreign Affairs the historian K. Krofta and the French ambassador to Prague, Charles Roux.

A month later was a great day for the Czech Club: Čapek, Fischer, Tille, Majerová and Pujmanová welcomed Thomas Mann. The German writers of Prague were of course present – Baum, Brod, Urzidil and Winder – as well as fifty other guests. It was a foretaste of the time when Prague would offer refuge to German intellectuals persecuted by the Nazis – until the fateful March of 1939.

Times were changing. Thomas Mann was greeted by His Excellency the German Ambassador to Prague just as Gerhardt Hauptmann was received the following October by the German Cultural Attaché. This was 1932, when the Berlin PEN Club was stilll capable of protesting through Schmidt-Pauli and Elster when writers were victimized for their political views. Otokar Fischer presented Mann and Hauptmann to an audience of leading Czech and German writers as the protagonists of the great ideals of German civilization. Who could have guessed that before long Mann would be an outcast and Czechoslovakia his refuge, readily granting him citizenship?

What was to come was terrible and tragic, but for the moment, wit, charm and amusing conversation were supreme, an optimism that found expression in the plays of Marcel Achard, so popular with the Czechs at that time. As a PEN dinner guest he was welcomed not only by critics Tille, Götz and Kodíček, but by those masters of the stage, Hilar, Honzl, Kohout and Steimar. Indeed, throughout the spring of 1932 it was the French flag that flew over Prague. A few days before Achard, Jerome Tharaud came; his work in collaboration with his brother Jean had much in common with that of Čapek in its psychological treatment of characters and in the outcome of the plot. At dinner he was joined by Tille and Konrád of the PEN Club as well as Hubert Beuve-Méry and Josef Palivec. Two weeks later the learned Léon Brunswig and André Lichtenberger arrived, greeted by O. Fischer, H. Jelínek, V. Tille, Emanuel Rádl and Jan Patočka.

Twelve days after the visit of Gerhardt Hauptmann, the Czech Club welcomed the well-known Norwegian novelist Johan

Boyer, followed at the end of January by Jean-Richard Bloch, author of the enchanting *Kurdish Nights*. Then came Arnold Zweig, novelist of the *Great White Man's War*. Visitors to Prague were still chosen for their literary stature and diversity.

We were now in 1933, when John Galsworthy, recent Nobel Prize winner and head of the International PEN Club, was dying and would not be able to chair the Dubrovnik Congress in June. May 18 was an ominous date – the day the Nazis made a public bonfire of books by many great German writers.

The Congress in Dubrovnik (25–28th May) confirmed H. G. Wells in the chair, and welcomed in its midst the Indian PEN Club led by Rabindranath Tagore. By this time there were over forty national PEN Clubs, and Wells was trying in vain to get one going in the USSR. This gathering of writers was thus a dignified stage for world intellectual opinion to forestall and outshine the politicians. The official delegation of the Berlin Club made an ostentatious exit when Ernst Toller, already in exile, appealed to the world to protest against the burning of books, sending writers to prison (Renn, Osietzky, Muhsam, Duncker, Witfogel) and banning musicians, such as Bruno Walter, Klemperer, Weil, Busch and Eisler, while graphic artists like Käthe Kollwitz, Otto Dix, Paul Klee, Max Liebermann and Hofer were silenced. Let the facts speak for themselves: by a decisive majority the Congress passed a resolution condemning what was happening in Germany as an attack not only on writers but on intellectual freedom altogether. It stressed the need to protect culture under all circumstances, and to bring nations closer together precisely through the diversity of their cultures. It explicitly condemned religious and racial prejudice and national fanaticism.

A. M. Tilschová and F. Langer of the Prague Club naturally voted for the resolution; with them in Dubrovnik were V. Červinka, M. Majerová, Husek, Muller, Tichý and Gejza Vámoš. H. G. Wells was invited to the Prague PEN Congress to be held in 1938.

The politicians could have taken their cue from the Dubrovnik PEN Congress, and it was not the fault of the writers that this did not happen. Principles did not have to be changed, but action was essential. The international executive committee meeting in London on November 8–9 decided that the German PEN Clubs could no longer claim membership in International PEN, while German writers in exile were offered membership in the English Club, or national clubs wherever they had found refuge. This was not possible in Czechoslovakia because the rules for membership called for Czechoslovak citizenship; nevertheless many intellectuals found refuge and support in their exile in our country, and when that help came to an end it was not by the decision of Czechoslovak democracy.

Internal conflicts grew sharper as the year progressed, under pressure of events in neighboring Nazi Germany, and not only among Germans living in the country. Nationalist and racial trouble broke out in the University at the beginning of the winter semester when the university insignia were due to be handed over to the Czech University of Prague by the German University. Aided and abetted by the chancellor, Domin, ultra-right-wing students started a pogrom against their left-wing colleagues which spread into the streets with the slogan "Out with the Jews!" Law-abiding citizens were abused and there were vandal attacks on the avant-garde Mánes art gallery and on the anti-fascist theater of Voskovec and Werich. The Czech admirers of Hitler and fascism wore a large capital N on the armbands of their grey shirts, for "Nic než národ," "Nothing but the nation." Their democratic opponents organized meetings in defense of democracy and freedom, addressed by writers, artists, university professors – and of course PEN Club members. The N thugs clearly lacked public support.

Two very different writers were guests of the Club in May. Jakob Wasserman, already an exile, met with Max Brod and others of like mind, while a week earlier it was Louis-Ferdinand Céline with whom the Czech writers enjoyed one of their most animated and delightful evenings. The author of *Descent Into the Depths of the Night* had not yet become a traitor and collaborator with the Nazis.

That autumn Karel Čapek came forward with a novel proposal. Himself the author of a notable translation of modern French verse, he could not agree with the supercilious attitude of some writers towards translators. He proposed that a committee should be set up to encourage the translation of Czech works and their propagation abroad. There were many translators abroad with considerable knowledge of the Czech language and interest in Czech writing, but no financial backing. The committee would provide such translators with an advance. The proposal was accepted, and Hanuš Jelínek, Václav Tille, Otto Pick and Jiřina Tůmová were chosen to form the committee. Before long considerable sums were sent by President Beneš and the head of the Živnobanka, Dr. Preis.

This marked the end of Karel Čapek's period as chairman of the PEN Club, and this time he would not be dissuaded from resigning. His place was taken by A. M. Tilschová, while František Kubka replaced Edmond Konrád as secretary.

Another year of important visitors began with Max Reinhardt who came in March, followed later by the poet Dorothy Wrench, Philippe Soupault, André Germain and Heinrich Mann, and then by the Nobel Prize winner Luigi Pirandello in December. The death of Mrs. Dawson-Scott in November was a severe blow to all those in the Czech PEN Club.

On February 27, 1935, the Club proudly celebrated its first ten years of life, remembering what Karel Čapek had said at its founding: "the Club will be what its members make of it." The International PEN Congress of 1938 was already on the horizon, and a special fund was set up to prepare for it, starting with a donation of 10,000 crowns from the President of the Republic and another 30,000 crowns from the Ministry of Foreign Affairs.

Events at home and abroad moved the Club to invite F. X. Šalda to lecture on "The Writer and Public Life" to an audience of critics and literary historians as well as writers. It was a good year, too, for international contacts. In March Salvador di Madariago, the prophet of European unity, came; then the heads of the Bucharest opera, Georgescu and Prodan, followed by several Scandinavian visitors, Erik Blomberg and Gunnar Ekelof of Sweden and Peter Jendorf Jensen of Norway. Ben van Eiselstein of Holland was followed by the French playwright

H. R. Lenormand, the last in a long list of visitors from all over Europe.

The following year was important for the life of the Czech Club. On April 8th, Božena Benešová died, no more than sixty-three years old, after ten years in the important though seemingly insignificant post of treasurer. Edmond Konrád represented the Czech Club at the Paris Congress, and we were honored that both the French and the English Clubs proposed Karel Čapek as successor to the outgoing chairman, H. G. Wells. Čapek accepted, but asked for a respite; he was due to marry Olga Scheinpflugová that year.

Early the following year the Yiddish writer Sholem Asch was a guest of honor, then the Romanian playwright Victor Eftimiu, followed in March by the French writer Eugene Dabit, author of the popular *Hotel du Nord*. To commemorate the centenary of the death of the Czech Romantic poet Karel Hynek Mácha there was a lecture by Jan Mukařovský. Two unusual names then appeared in the list of guests, the playwright Vsevolod Višnevski and the film producer Ephim Djigan, who were then working on "We of Kronstadt."

The French poet and critic Emile Henriot, the novelist and essayist Henri Bordeaux and his colleague Jean Prévost added to the long list of French visitors in May and June, while Claude Haughton from England and Gudmundur Kamban from Iceland show how broadly the PEN Club threw its nets. The visit of Dr. Elsa West-Neuhard, a well-known Danish writer and translator of Czech prose, augured well for the future of Czech writing abroad.

Lack of funds prevented the Czech Club from sending a delegation to the Buenos Aires Congress in September, but we were represented by the Czech ambassador, Dr. Kadeřábek. Karel Čapek could not be elected to the chairmanship as he was not present, and the Czech vote went to support Jules Romains.

Memorial evenings for those who died during the year were held for the Czech plawright Jaroslav Hilbert and for Dezsó Kosztolány, G. K. Chesterton and Luigi Pirandello.

That year, 1936, the Slovak writers organized a Congress in Trenčianské Teplice, where guidelines for the Society of Slovak

Writers were laid down. There was one clear line: cooperation
with Czech writers on the basis of equality, a conclusion which
would have been reached with difficulty by a common Czech and
Slovak meeting, but which was most welcome in Prague. The
Czech delegation of Tilschová, Majerová, Hora, Jelínek and Kopta made an excellent impression with their open-minded discussions with their Slovak colleagues (making no attempt to solve
their problems for them). It is true that the Czechs were glad the
question of union was not at the fore, for starting from scratch to
reach the international horizon, Czech writers would be there
too, as the critic Bedřich Václavek commented.

The time was not ripe for a congress in Czechoslovakia of
German-speaking writers, for political reasons. No society can
speak up when there is no responsible voice to be heard. We can
listen, though, to that of Rudolf Fuchs, poet, critic and translator
of Czech poetry, a member of the Czech PEN Club. He was addressing the Bertold Brecht Club in Prague in February 1936,
words that were all the more significant as their audience was
one of German writers living in Czechoslovakia. His historical
account of German writing bore on the present state of affairs in
Czechoslovakia, and many great names were spoken: Stifter,
Rilke, Kafka, Brod, Werfel, Kisch, Winder, but also Watzlik,
Muhlberger and Kolbenheyer. This last had been awarded a
Czechoslovak State Prize. "He accepted the prize," Fuchs went
on, "only to protest a few weeks later that he was not a Czechoslovak German but an 'Alemannic.' German nationality has little to feed its poets on in Czechoslovakia, regarding them as
cosmopolitans if they will not write according to the rules of
blubo." [From the German *Blut und Boden*, blood and soil, a
Nazi concept.] Fuchs saw the difference between Czech and
German poetry in that the former was turned in on itself while
the latter gazed out into the world. German poets in Czechoslovakia suffered because of their national characteristics; what
they wrote had nothing to do with the country they lived in or
the people around them. Recalling the funeral of Czech writer
Svatopluk Čech, Fuchs said: "Remember Rilke dying in Switzerland, ten years ago last November. We heard about it from the

newspapers. Did anyone from the Czechoslovak-German Society for Science and the Arts bother to lay a wreath on his grave? Anyone from the German Writers Union, Concordia? Anyone from the German University in Prague, from any German club or society here? Not a soul."

"The Germans in the Šumava, in the Ore Mountains, in the Giant Mountains, in Moravia and Silesia have turned their gaze – this is a well-known fact and I want to stress its literary implications here – not inwards to their own souls but outwards and away."

Fuchs concluded with the sad words of someone from the other camp, the chairman of the German Writers Union in Czechoslovakia, Alfred Scholz, writing in the *Sudetendeutsche Schriftsteller*: "The spiritual misery of our Sudeten German people is no less than their material poverty, but the sad consequences are not yet obvious. Spiritual poverty grows unobserved and gnaws at the creative energy of individuals and the whole nation. That is why we need spiritual help."

Fuchs' short study was a significant contribution during those months when clear-sighted analyses were few on either the Czech or the German side. Above all, he tried to go beyond the empty phrases of the day and find the reality beneath. It was an eloquent call, but it fell on deaf ears.

There were plenty of problems to be solved, but no one dared or was capable of seeing that we had reached the end of the road. The end of two or even of three distinct literary identities side by side in the same country. Yet to admit that this was what lay ahead meant accepting the real Nazi threat that Czech culture must be destroyed, and the existing Nazi practice of destroying not only Jewish culture but the Jewish people as well. That was too apocalyptic a vision to be faced.

Yet the apocalypse has become a familiar phenomenon in modern Europe. It is natural that the human mind resists the idea of the apocalypse, preferring to seek comfort and good cheer – a positive illusion, so to speak. And yet...

The thirties were not so far removed from the first world war, yet already the illusion that war was past and done with had faded. Democracy was no longer the sole accepted ideal, and it was calmly accepted that here and there democracy could be attacked and destroyed.

Both these attitudes could be seen during the Spanish Civil War, when a handful of generals overthrew the democratically elected government in the summer of 1936. There followed three years of murderous fighting which ended in the establishment of a murderous dictatorship – for the next thirty-five years.

One of the effects of the war was to drive intellectuals into exile, and after the wave of German refugees came the Spanish and Catalonians. J. R. Jimenez, L. Felipe, J. Guillen, M. Aub, R. Alberti and others fled abroad or were not allowed to return home, like Picasso and Casals, not to mention those who were killed, like Lorca, Machado or Hernandez. In Prague Albert, Camus greeted Salvador di Madariaga on his seventieth birthday with the words: "You have chosen exile in order to testify to the truth." The eloquent truth these exiles proclaimed passed unheard by the powers that be, however, and thanks to their support Franco's clerical fascism held the reins of power from 1939 until 1974. The exiled writers were fortunate in that there are many Spanish-speaking countries in the world.

The Spanish Civil War saw intellectuals in the democratic countries united as never before, liberals of all shades of opinion alongside left-wingers of all kinds. Yet it was during this Spanish war that a fateful rift began to gape. Malraux, Spender, Paz, Hemingway, Silone and others moved to a highly critical position, and the disruptive force did not stem from the ostrich policy of non-intervention practiced by the western democracies, but from the Soviet policy of Great Russian imperialism combined with Stalin's unprincipled dogmatism. The boundless admiration of many western intellectuals for the "land of the victorious revolution" of which they had no firsthand experience faded as knowledge grew. Significantly and in characteristic fashion it was the "Return from the Soviet Union" of André Gide that was the bombshell. As the time of the international congress in Prague drew nearer, Edmond Konrád published an article in *Přítomnost* entitled "The Political History of the PEN Club." The Club's "history" had lacked such a commentary and the eve of

the Congress was certainly a well-chosen moment. The author
began by saying that "the very title of these remarks seems a
contradiction in terms, for the aims of the PEN Club could be
said to be anti-political and their origin in "dining clubs" where
writers meet at the dinner table and get to know one another,
perfectly innocent." He went on to speak of the widespread family one "mother," Mrs. Dawson-Scott, had founded across the
world, crossing political and other frontiers, and maneuvering
between the two major currents of the day, fascism and communism. He concluded: "Let these be slight indications of the political preoccupations forced on literature today, forced on writers
whose goals are nonpolitical. The moment literature becomes
politics the nonpolitical stand is itself a political statement. Totalitarianism, leaving no room for privacy of the individual,
turns writers into political creatures, for it is their task to preserve the continuity of the animal known as man in the face of
autarchy and totalitarianism, to preserve the human dimensions of man, and to save truth for the world."

It was of course impossible to maintain a nonpolitical organization in a political world, and indeed questionable whether the
attempt to "preserve the human dimensions of man" and "save
truth for the world" could be anything but political. It was also
far from easy to see through this illusion of nonpolitical activity
so long as "political" was taken to mean extremism and extreme
views, as though there were no other "political" attitude. For the
history of the PEN Club, the 1933 Congress in Dubrovnik was a
turning point; it had become necessary to to expel three Clubs of
writers belonging to a great European nation, because they
trampled the PEN Charter underfoot. From that time on, nonpolitical activity in the PEN Clubs could only be illusory. Yet a nonpolitical stand did exist; it had always been possible to be political while avoiding extremist views, and it would always be so.
The Prague Congress confirmed this, in all aspects of its proceedings.

Long before the event, the Czech Club had the foresight to set
up a fund to cover the expenses of the Congress, and it was
equally prudent on the intellectual plane. Otherwise it would
not have been possible to publish so exacting a volume as *At the*

European Crossroads: A Historical Sketch of Democratic Ideas in Czechoslovakia, in English and French. The contributors were all acknowledged experts: the historian Václav Chaloupecký dealt with "the time of kings and princes" in sixteen chapters; František Hruby described a tragic period of Czech history in his "Hapsburgs and Czechs during the Reformation and Counter-Reformation"; while the theologian J. L. Hromádka sketched "The Heritage of the Czech Reformation" and Professor Albert Pražák covered literary history from the beginning of the revival in the last century to the present day, (to 1938), in his "Spirit of Modern Czech Literature." These scholarly chapters were introduced by Karel Čapek, while Ferdinand Peroutka brought the volume to a close with his "Portrait of Czechoslovak Democracy." The purpose of these scholarly pages was to show the world that things were not muddled and confused at this crossroads of Europe, but that it was the historical home of a nation that had been there for over a thousand years with its language and its culture, and with its political identity, its state. This book set out boldly to refute the idea prevalent in some western capitals that here was an unknown people not worth going to war for, not worth risking peace, as Neville Chamberlain shamelessly declared as he played the principal villain of the Munich agreement later that year.

While the scholars dealt with history, Čapek and Peroutka applied their conclusions to the contemporary scene. "To be here in the heart of Europe has always meant being dragged into every conflict that has arisen throughout history," wrote Čapek, and continued, "Throughout their history the Czech people have had to face two problems: in the first place, how to defend themselves and their frontiers at whatever cost, taking up arms to do so; and in the second place, how to forge alliances and treaties to take them out of their historical isolation; in other words, to follow a policy of what is now called European cooperation."

It would have been difficult for the Czech PEN Club to evolve its own theory of Czech history, but it was clear to those who read this volume that the Club followed the line of Palacký and Masaryk. This can be seen for instance in the fact that J. L. Hromádka, Professor of Theology at the Jan Hus Faculty, was en-

trusted with the history of both the Reformation and the Counter-Reformation, clearly an echo of the views held up at the
Prague Castle, the intellectual atmosphere around the President. Nor is it illogical that those Catholics whose voices went
unheard should come out after Munich with harsh criticism of
the First Republic and of course of the PEN Club.

Preparations for the Congress meanwhile went on apace, in
the optimistic belief that democracy could still be saved and that
it would be unsporting to insinuate otherwise. On June 6, 1938,
the delegates and guests met in the Salla Terrena of the Wald-
stein Palace; everything functioned. Seventy official delegates
were expected to stay for six days, as well as the four hundred
guests. Two theater performances had been sold-out and there
were outings prepared, with fifteen teams of guides, transportation organized, and souvenirs ready. The original estimate for
expenses was 200,000 crowns, of which 40,000 crowns would
come from the Congress Fund and 100,000 from the government, and there were no fears that the remaining 60,000 crowns
would not be forthcoming. The honorary chairman had accepted,
the hospitality and transportation committees were functioning,
and a Ladies' Committee made up of leading social figures led by
Mrs. Rottová was poised for action. Above all, this Prague Congress could offer a unique experience: the Sokol mass gymnastic
displays and triumphal processions in traditional costumes
through the streets of the capital were a guarantee of enthusiastic crowds to overcome the reserve of critical intellectuals and
ensure that they would take home with them the firm impression of active and effective democracy in Czechoslovakia.

"Our Prague Congress is a reality," Jules Romains said in his
opening speech on June 7th in the Law Faculty of Charles University, the oldest in Central Europe, "In June 1938 these words
are eloquent in themselves." At this point Romains showed his
sense of history: "Let us recall what our feelings were in Buenos
Aires in 1936 – civil war had just broken out in Spain. Who
would not have said at the time that this war of ideological passions, as it was thought to be, might well start a blaze throughout Europe that could spread to the world at large." Perhaps
Romains was not attempting an apologia for the policy of non-

intervention that gave Franco's clerical fascism the victory in Spain, so much as justifying the optimism with which he viewed the explosive situation in Czechoslovakia. Perhaps – for he ended his speech with the hope that "at this moment in a fine June 1938, a new era has begun for Czechoslovakia," a new era of peace and prosperity, that is to say.

The Congress went on, speeches were made including one by Prime Minister Milan Hodža, which received worldwide praise. The PEN Club members proceeded with their own program, as the *Prager Tagblatt* reported:

"Two committees met yesterday to discuss practical proposals for different kinds of literature and for their distribution. Today's plenary session will hear summaries of the committee's recommendations.

The first committee, chaired by the French writer Luc Durtain, dealt with the relations between folk and 'literary' writing. One of the speakers was Karel Čapek, who quoted typical modern writers in support of his view of the poet and prose writer as combatants for a better atmosphere for creative writing. Never before, he said in conclusion, had literature had such a tragic and heroic opportunity for greatness as in our difficult times. Čapek was followed in the discussion by Horák, Mukařovský, Nevinson (England), Byrne (Ireland), Dimitriyevich (Yugoslavia), Taveros Pastos (Brazil), Dunčev (Bulgaria) and Schottman (Holland).

The second committee was concerned with writing for young people, and was chaired by Herman Ould (England). Marie Majerová and Hana Gregorová-Tajovská spoke for Czechoslovakia, Herzfeld for the German writers' group from London, Ellis Williams (England), Claude Aveline (France), Cioculescu (Romania), Rutter (England) and others.

The third committee discussed modern means of transmission, including radio, film and television. Edmond Konrád spoke, and Marie Kuncewiczova of Poland explained their attempt at a 'spoken novel.' Dr. Jan Löwenbach of Czechoslovakia also discussed this subject."

These professional questions could not of course overshadow the political significance of the Congress. The mood was exuberant, but when Karel Čapek ended the reception in the Černín

Palace of the Foreign Ministry with the words "we have won all along the line," he was expressing the mood and not giving a sober analysis of the situation. Friendly encouragement and delighted enchantment with Czechoslovakia were well in evidence, but not unexpected, for as early as March that year French writers had organized an evening at International PEN headquarters attended by such stars as Paul Valéry, André Maurois and Luc Durtain, where Valéry had praised the honor and courage of Czech soldiers, referring to the Siberian legions, as the conservative press noted. There was truth in what he said, however, and he then concluded with the words: "This is a nation whose friends we are and will always be, with no fear that they might abuse this friendship or that they might act madly. They are not fond of crazy acts. This is a people truly beloved of Minerva."

Jules Romains added nothing to this praise of the Czechs, except advice which might have thrown some doubt on Minerva's wisdom in approving them: "Be wise and conciliatory; act with a good conscience. Be honorable to the point of magnanimity. Take care not to seem ungracious, but be equally careful not to overdo cleverness, for in a few years it might destroy the little that remains of international ethics, the little mutual respect that still remains between nations. If we are reasonable, firm and loyal, we earn the respect of our partners even against their will, and the support of the whole world, which still matters."

It is worth noting that the Catalonians present responded by saying that "the Catalonians were not fighting only for the right to be free and not political slaves, the right to live in a just society and not in social injustice, but for their very existence as a people. Defeated, the Catalonians would be subjected to the most dangerous attack in their history, aimed at destroying them economically while eradicating their name, their national identity and the language which has served to express their thoughts and feelings for centuries."

It is perhaps worth recalling what Romains said of the two wars already being waged: "We cannot be content with the manner in which war is being waged in Spain and in China, from the spiritual standpoint we are here to defend." The manner in which war is being waged... but no word of the causes or of any responsibility.

Nevertheless the Prague Congress met, and important people from all over the world were there. The Prague committee responsible for the Congress consisted of A. M. Tilschová, Karel Čapek, František Langer, J. Hrdinová as treasurer, and B. Havránek, H. Jelínek, E. Konrád, K. Krejčí, F. Kubka, M. Majerová, V. Neff, J. Palivec, O. Pick, E. Rippl, J. Šusta, and J. Tůmová. About two hundred writers came to Prague from all over the world, from Argentina, Belgium, Bulgaria, Catalonia, Croatia, England, Finland, France, Holland, Israel, Latvia, Lithuania, Poland, Serbia and Slovenia. Famous names like Crémieux, Durtain, Thérive, Aveline, Piérrard, Fabricius, van Friesland, Herman Ould, Nevinson, Wells, Begovich, Albracht and Djorić were among those present, yet others were absent. All those present applauded the Prime Minister when he gave literature the same weight as the army in creating a new state, and called for constructive nationalism in international relations. From all sides came expressions of solidarity with Czechoslovakia, or at least sympathy with her aims, even from the Italian PEN Club (T. F. Marinetti), but above all from the small northern nations – and most fervently from Yugoslavia.

In an interview for the Polish *Nowy Dziennik* of Cracow, Karel Čapek sounded the right note: "The Congress was held in an atmosphere of fraternal understanding, which is saying a lot in these troubled times, but if the influence of literature on life is what we are thinking of," he added, "writers cannot be subjected to pressure at a time when force has the upper hand in political life, when brutality is more powerful than the spirit. At such a time writers and intellectuals cannot exert much influence."

Time passed, and the euphoria of June slowly dissolved in the oppressive atmosphere of the run-up to what was committed solely at the expense of one small Central European country, the "bastion of democracy" (the subtitle of the book *On the Crossroads of Europe*). The writers of this small country, already cognizant of Great Power tactics, were not to be lulled with fair words. Less than three months after the Prague Congress they met again, to appeal "to the conscience of the world" in a manifesto which said among other things:

"We appeal to you, who are entitled above all others to defend that which has up to now been the hallmark and the pride of Europe and the whole civilized world: respect for the truth, for intellectual freedom – and a clear conscience. We ask you to come and judge for yourselves who it is that is moved by an honest desire for peace and justice, and who in lust for conquest is resorting to lies and violence. We ask you, writers, to explain to your countrymen that we, a small peace-loving country situated at the most dangerous outpost of Europe, are doomed to fight, and that this cruel battle will be fought not only for our own survival, but for you, too, and for the moral and spiritual values proclaimed by the free and peace-loving peoples of the world. Let no one be prey to illusion: after us it will be the turn of other peoples and other lands. We call upon all writers, all intellectuals and all who have faith in the human spirit, to use all possible means to bring this truth home to all peoples. In the name of the Association of Czechoslovak Writers..."

Of the names signed below this appeal, the first, Josef Čapek, and the last, Vladislav Vančura, were the names of men who gave their lives in the struggle they foretold. Half of the thirty signatories were members of the PEN Club, but that is not what matters. At such moments people are united or divided by the truth they acknowledge and by their conscience. It can never be known how many writers read this appeal in the last days before the Munich agreement of September 30, 1938, was signed, but many who had never read it nevertheless turned out into the streets of Belgrade, Zagreb, Lublyana and other towns in the Yugoslavia that no longer exists today, sending great waves of support for the people of Czechoslovakia. It might be thought that writers and their manifestos ought to follow the dictates of the street, but the experience of these days when those same people are killing each other for their "differentness" destroys this new – or revived old – illusion.

One thing is certain: happy the day when no manifesto is called for.

On September 30, 1938, the intellectuals of Czechoslovakia met again to issue a manifesto addressed to the whole world, questioning the joy that greeted the proclamation of "peace in our time" and showing up the lie beneath the promise of Munich, which in fact crippled a living people, robbed it of its natural resources, its industrial potential, its communication system, leaving it no hope of self-defense.

"Never did we think that the civilized world would allow violence to conquer right in such a naked and shameless fashion as the four Great Powers have used against us, not even letting us know. Never did we think that international guarantees could so lightly be thrust aside. It is not only our own fate but that of Europe that is at stake, and the fate of all those small European states whose very existence depends on the inviolability of an ethical code. That is why we appeal to the conscience of those whose decisions can shake the very foundations of European civilization. Do not forget that the violation of the weak, treachery and cowardice can never bring real peace, permanent, honorable peace. Speaking for Czech and Slovak intellectuals, we here declare that we will never relinquish our historic right to our land, to a free life there, and to a reasonable degree of economic prosperity despite our submission to overpowering force. You must accept that it is your duty to give battle on the side of real peace, a peace that would ensure life and rights to all. Rest assured that otherwise the fate that awaits us will be yours, too, unless you can take an effective stand against the methods of violence and oppression which have been used against us."

This manifesto was signed by representatives of thirty-six institutions and organizations from all literary and artistic spheres, from the Academy of Sciences and Arts, to the Actors Club of the Prague Municipal Theaters. Thousands of intellectuals including, of course, members of the PEN Club, were among the signatories.

It was a voice calling in the wilderness, and in that silence one could but recall the voice of the Horse in the poem by Jaroslav Vrchlický, "Quiet Steps":

*"How I pity you, apostles of humanity, with your Peace
Congresses, your brochures and your slogans,
when first the horses are shot at experimentally,
so that later, people will be better targeted.
How I pity you. What are you looking for here?"*

In the run-up to the International PEN Congress, the Czech
Club was in the vanguard of the fight for Czechoslovak democracy, but after Munich it became the rearguard, defending the
retreat. These are military terms that have no place in literature, but here and at this moment they were apt indeed. Plans
were afoot to maintain links with the outer world under the very
nose of the Nazis, and to arrange for those intellectuals whose
lives were endangered to escape to freedom. Help from outside
was essential, and in London this came from Storm Jameson
and the PEN Club secretary Herman Ould; in Paris Benjamin
Crémieux was extremely helpful. The Director of the French
Institute in Prague, Alfred Fichelle, was the go-between, passing information and procuring visas. The Rev. Waitstill Sharp
was a tower of strength, getting Professor Kozák to safety and
helping many others. Some of the visas for France were not in
fact used, because some of those in danger refused to leave.
Others left illegally through Poland (like Eduard Goldstücker,
later a Czech PEN Club member). In all these attempts to save
the lives of Czech writers it was clear that the June Congress
had established the moral imperative.

Tens of thousands of ordinary citizens were forced to flee the
regions surrendered to Germany under the Munich agreement.
They were in dire need of help, yet at the same time the lowest
dregs came to the surface, attacking the principles of democracy
as the cause of defeat, attacking those who proclaimed and personified those principles, Masaryk, Beneš, Čapek and the intellectuals. *Vlajka, Arijský boj* and similar fascist gutter press rags
were in the forefront of the mud-slinging. Such filth had little
chance of convincing decent people, but Karel Čapek was certainly more profoundly wounded by ambitious attacks by intellectuals such as the article in the Catholic literary journal *Akord*,
entitled "A Broken Spirit," identifying the spirit of defeat not

only with the person of Karel Čapek but with his writings: "Even if Chamberlain's self-confidence stinks, enthralled by its own success, it cannot be justified before God. Before the nation it can easily be justified, for the arguments he uses to explain his policy are those put forward by Dr. Galen in (Čapek's) *White Plague.* This spirit has been defeated and our defeat is the fruit of that tree issued from seeds we ourselves have cast to the winds."

It is all the more relevant to quote these lines in our history of the PEN Club if we go on to quote the writer: "We have put our fate in the hands of Freemasons lodges, Rotary Clubs and PEN Clubs, yet why were none of these people able to do anything for us? Why, for example, did Jules Romains, chairman of the French PEN Club, who should have been one of the most responsible guardians and protectors of our national values, declare his profound satisfaction with the outcome of Munich?"

So far the article in *Akord* was right. What Jules Romains said after Munich contrasted painfully with his words before that date. Nor was he alone, alas. Another famous name appeared in the article by Jaroslav Zaorálek in *Přítomnost*: André Maurois, who had been an enthusiastic guest of the Czech PEN Club, wrote with great glee that Chamberlain would remain the immortal model of an honest politician, for at Munich he had fulfilled all his promises, both moral and practical.

One could quote many such examples of intellectual blindness or naivety, for the months before the outbreak of the second world war were among the most shameful in the whole of the twentieth century. Most monstrous of all, those who organized wholesale capitulation to Hitler were praised as far-sighted politicians and saviors of peace, while his helpless opponents along with all true defenders of democracy were blamed for a capitulation which they were helpless to prevent, and even for the dictators' aggression.

Articles like the one from *Akord* quoted here remain as evidence of a falsification of values. "Democracy failed because it had no confidence in itself," the writer went on, "and it lost confidence in itself because it refused to trust anything else. 'All power comes from the people!' Well, that power has been proved empty, and Nazism is the great mocking answer to such declarations." The intellectual and moral sophistry of this attack on democracy and on Karel Čapek, and its underhanded manipulation of the ideas of power, ethics and politics, are exposed in that one sentence. The writer went on: "It is certainly no mere chance that Karel Čapek is the author of a play in which robots destroy the human race while the New Man who is to people the earth is an industrial product injected with some sort of optimistic future."

The critic could not fail to see that this play was a warning of the dangers of the industrial spirit, but his aim was clear: "If we are to preserve our spiritual identity against the Germans we must raise the Cross of Christ against the swastika. The greatest danger threatening us today comes from the swastika, and there is no other defense against that."

For the *Akord's* commentator, Nazism was an ironic attack on the principle of democracy, but the real irony lies in the two crosses facing each other in combat, while in Spain under Franco's dictatorship they were happily collaborating, as they were to do shortly afterwards in the "independent" Slovak state established with Hitler's blessing.

Karel Čapek was unable to survive in this vicious atmosphere, and died at that sad Christmas when Czechoslovakia still existed on paper, but with something lacking. His death could be seen as the epitaph of the life of the Czech PEN Club – were it not for the brave men and women who carried its life with them into exile, into the heart of the battle against Nazism, and those equally courageous souls who kept its memory alive here at home, saving precious testimony from the grabbing hands of the Gestapo.

REPORT ON THE ACTIVITY
OF THE CZECHOSLOVAK PEN CLUB IN ENGLAND

"Late in 1940 members of the Czech and Slovak PEN Clubs living in England decided to revive their activities in exile. Led by the former vice-chairman František Langer, they visited the President of the Republic, Dr. Edward Beneš, who accepted the honor-

*ary chairmanship of the Club and promised moral and material
support for its activities in England.
    At the inaugural meeting František Langer was elected chair-
man, Josef Kodíček secretary, and Gustav Stern treasurer. Early
in 1941, however, Josef Kodíček was forced to resign under pressure of other work, and Viktor Fischl was elected in his place. The
committee was enlarged to include Josef Kodíček as vice-chairman and Julius Fürth as accountant. The committee then began
its work.
    On February 19, 1941, the Czechoslovak PEN Club invited the
members of the English PEN Club and writers of other countries
then living in England to a party at the Czechoslovak Institute,
which was attended by President Beneš and Mrs. Hana Benešová, and where the guests were welcomed by Jan Masaryk, the
Minister of Foreign Affairs. František Langer stressed that in
Czechoslovakia writers had always played a leading role in political life, and that both Presidents of the Republic had been
members of the PEN Club. Storm Jameson, who chaired the English PEN Club, was prevented from attending by illness, but her
speech was read by Herman Ould, general secretary of International PEN, along with an address sent by the former chairman
Henry Nevinson. Ernest Raymond spoke for the writers of England; his novel "The Last to Rest" gave fictional form to the atmosphere of the last International PEN Club Congress, in
Prague, in the year that led up to Munich. A musical program
was given by the Czech Trio.
    On May 19th the Club arranged a party together with the
Polish PEN Club, addressed by the chairman of the Polish Club,
Marja Kuncewiczowa, and Viktor Fischl. The music was again
provided by the Czech Trio.
    Another joint Polish-Czechoslovak event was a party at the
Institute where the guest of honor was J. Liddell Geddie, chairman of the Scottish Club, who had entertained František Langer
in Edinburgh shortly before. On this Scottish trip the chairman
spoke about Czechoslovak theater, and particularly amateur the-
atricals. Other speakers at the party were Antoni Slonimski and
Herman Ould; guests viewed an exhibition of photographs from
Czechoslovakia.*

On July 15, 1941, the members of the Czechoslovak PEN Club were invited to a dinner arranged by the English PEN Club for all the members of International PEN then living in England. It was agreed that the seventeenth International Congress would be held in London. The secretary of the Czechoslovak Club, Viktor Fischl, spoke.

Reports of these events, together with the speeches delivered, were published in full or summarized in the PEN News.

August 1941 was entirely taken up with preparations for the International Congress; the chairman and secretary attended all meetings of the international committee making technical arrangements. The committee also had to come to terms with the delicate matter of the future chairmanship of International PEN since it was clear that Jules Romains would have to be removed from that office.

The Czechoslovak Club elected František Langer and Viktor Fischl as delegates to the Seventeenth International PEN Congress, while the President of the Republic, honorary chairman of the Club, sent an address which was printed in the Congress proceedings. To mark the occasion the Czechoslovak Club printed a special issue of the magazine "The Spirit of Czechoslovakia." Josef Kodíček chaired the Congress session on September 12th, and the following day made a speech on the writer's responsibility to the public, which was also published in the proceedings. Books by members of the Czechoslovak PEN Club which had been published after the outbreak of war were on show.

The last social event of the year was a party given by the Polish and Czechoslovak PEN Clubs at which the guest of honor was André Labarthe, publisher of "La France Libre." He gave a talk on the present state of French literature.

We began 1942 with an afternoon devoted to T. S. Eliot, arranged in cooperation with the English PEN Club. Professor Bonamy Dobrée spoke about the poet who then himself read his poem "East Coker." A Czech translation by PEN Club member Libuše Pánková was read by Juraj Slávik, accompanied by music by Vilem Tausky.

A new committee was elected on February 24, 1942, and functioned until the present day (10. 11. 1945):

Chairman: František Langer
Vice-chairmen: Juraj Slávik and Josef Kodíček
Secretary: Viktor Fischl
Treasurer: Gustav Stern
Accountants: Julius Firt and Gustav Winter

A special committee was elected at this meeting to elaborate a program of lectures on Czechoslovak intellectual life as viewed by those who had spent some years abroad. The following lectures were given:

Josef Kodíček: Literary Life
Hubert Ripka: Journalism
František Langer: The Way We Live
Gustav Winter: What Our Intellectual Life Looks Like To Someone Viewing It "Through Western Eyes"

Czechoslovaks living in London found the lectures so attractive that the PEN Club decided to arrange a further series that year and in 1943, entitled "We and the world." The following talks were given:

4. 9. 42: We and France, by Gustav Winter
18. 9: We and England, by M. Weatherall
16. 10: We and Russia, by Prokop Maxa
30. 10: We and the Germans, by Jaroslav Stránský
7. 12: We and America, by Jan Masaryk
11. 1. 1943: We and the Hungarians, by Vlado Clementis
J. L. Hromádka brought the series to an end with a lecture entitled "What is our spiritual life moving towards?"

These lectures were very much appreciated by the Czechoslovaks living in London, who took advantage of the opportunity to join in the discussions. The PEN Club did not neglect the need to maintain and enhance contacts with the writers of other countries living in exile in England. In the course of 1943 two major meetings were arranged with English writers and others from the Allied literary world.

*In 1944 Professor Otakar Odložil lectured on "The Two Faces
of America" and later another series of talks was given on the
place of writers in the public life of their respective countries.
William Saroyan spoke on writers in America, Kaminski of the
"Soviet War News" talked about writers in his country, while
Phyllis Bentley discussed writers in English public life. The PEN
Club also arranged several film screenings, with a reception, il-
lustrating life in Czechoslovakia.*

*That year the Club finally organized a lecture by T. S. Eliot,
together with the Czechoslovak Institute; he spoke about the individuality of each national culture and the intellectual unity of
Europe. A lecture by Edwin Muir on the spirit of modern English
literature was also arranged. Together with the Institute the Club
had previously organized a lecture by the Dutch writer Johan
Fabricius on folk theater in Malaya.*

*After the tragedy of Lidice, the Club's editorial committee pre-
pared a book about Lidice to which writers of many countries
contributed and which published the protests and condolences
which poured into the PEN Club from all over the world. Members all received the book, which was otherwise soon sold out.*

*The PEN Club held a memorial evening for Vladislav Vanču-
ra, and honored the memory of other members who had died
during the war: Gustav Winter, Otto Pick, Rudolf Fuchs, Arne
Laurin and Karel Kříž.*

*The Czechoslovk PEN Club had its center in England, but
many writers spent the war years in America, and had their contacts with the PEN Club there. František Langer, as we have noted, visited the Scottish PEN Club, while the secretary visited the
Club in Northern Ireland. Club members were regularly invited
to other PEN centers in London.*

*This is a simple, and perhaps not absolutely complete account
of what we did during the war years. Allow me to conclude this
dry report by expressing my conviction that we were not idle, that
we used those five years to get to understand something of the
spirit of English life, and that we made warm and valuable
friendships with English writers and those of other countries.
Perhaps we could have done more, but I know that we were considered one of the most active of the exile PEN Clubs in London.*

I am sure we brought no shame on the good name of the Czecho-slovak PEN Club and with a clear conscience we will make way for the leadership to be elected at home."

Viktor Fischl wrote his report by the Thames, and he read it where the Vltava flowed past the tall windows of Mánes, in the Artists Club which succeeded the Czech and German Theatrical Club, an organization set up in a spirit of cooperation. Under the Nazi occupation the Artists Club was the stronghold of intellectual insubordination. Many wonderful people contributed to the Club's cultural programs, which miraculously escaped the notice of the Gestapo and their informers – scholars and artists like Zdeněk Wirth, Albert Pražák, Václav Vydra, Jan Port, Lubomír Linhart, B. Půlpánová and Vladimír Žikeš. No bullets pierced the Club' s windows during the May uprising, nor did the February bombs that devastated the nearby Emaus monastery damage the Club's walls.

It was November 1945, and the Czech intellectual atmosphere was still that of anti-Nazi unity, while only those who had had no interest in belonging during the Nazi occupation kept apart, more inclined to preserve the spirit of the moldering Second Republic.

At the end of May the large Lucerna hall filled up to listen to Zdeněk Nejedlý, just back from exile in the Soviet Union. With S. K. Neumann in the chair, he recapitulated and put forward what was to become the official program. The stress he laid on the Pan-Slavic and Russophile character of the struggle against the Nazis, with its assumption of Soviet hegemony, was the first hint of the Stalin-Zhdanov conception of culture, but the threat it implied was perhaps clear only to those who noticed the stress laid on true international understanding by some of the Czech speakers.

By presidential decree, organizations prohibited by the Nazis were able to renew their activities automatically, without waiting for official permission, and the PEN Club was unquestionably one of these. A plenary meeting was therefore called for November 10, 1945, in Mánes; it was the first post-war meeting of the Club, attended by twenty-three members and by Storm Jameson as a guest.

A. M. Tilschová, in the chair, opened with a speech which we give here in full:

"We meet here today in our twentieth anniversary year, after a long and enforced silence. On April 17, 1942, the Gestapo dissolved the Club, and even before that we were prevented from doing anything in our own country, not to speak of prohibited foreign contacts. Jiřina Tůmová, a loyal colleague, will give you a detailed account of how we proceeded during the years of the war and the German occupation; she carried out her duties as secretary with remarkable perspicacity and selfless devotion, beginning twenty-three years ago when our meetings were held in the home of Karel Čapek in the Little Quarter. Alas, our joyful reunion lies under a cloud, like a lovely bouquet of flowers beneath a black veil: no other organization suffered such cruel losses during the war as our Club. Between the cheering Sokol crowds whose enthusiasm brought the Czech PEN Club Congress to a close just before Munich, and the rebirth of the Republic this year, lies a chasm and an abyss, a wound that will not heal. It festers with the sufferings of the finest laborers sent to cultivate the vineyards of Czech culture.

The bare figures are eloquent enough: over forty of our one hundred and twenty members, more than a third, were persecuted, arrested, imprisoned and executed. We can thank God that some of those selected for liquidation in the planned destruction of Czech culture survived by lucky chance, and as it were, miraculously. I am happy that with our Nestor Jaroslav Kvapil, other writers have returned: K. J. Beneš, Václav Černý, František Bořek-Dohalský, Jan Hájek, Miloš Jirko, Karek Krejčí, František Kubka, Zdeněk Němeček, Josef Palivec and Lev Sychrava. Two courageous women also survived, Naděžda Papoušková and Jiřina Tůmová, both of them having suffered not only imprisonment in Pankrác jail but personal tragedy as well.

I ask you to stand and honor the memory of those who have not survived to return to us. Death took a terrible harvest in our small circle! Some seemed to die a peaceful death, yet their premature departure came with the whirlwind that raged over Europe, tearing them up by the roots even in their homeland. The first such victim of Nazism was the poet Otokar Fischer, who suffered a stroke as the Germans occupied Austria. In the heavy days of the first Christmas of the Second Republic, Karel Čapek died, the friend of Masaryk, too fragile and defenseless despite his optimistic declarations. Soon after the May revolution the pale flame of Václav Hora's lyric inspiration was extinguished, and it is no solace to us that his coffin could be draped in the Czechoslovak flag. Vilém Mathesius is no longer with us, with his philosophical smile even in illness; Hanuš Jelínek did not live to see the longed for moment when "the reins of government are once more in your hands, oh Czechs!" We are desolate from the unredeemed tragedy of Šusta; Vincenc Červinka died, Čenkov-Stehlík, Ljacky, and at last death sent for that lover of the dance, Siblín. There were many who were not allowed to die in their homeland: Karel Fragner, Otto Pick, Rudolf Fuchs the translator of Bezruč, Arne Laurin and our excellent Winter all died in far-off lands. May the earth lie light upon them!

The darkness of concentration camps and prisons. The silent pilgrim, and so much our own, Josef Čapek, disappeared into the German unknown, the two elderly friends Arnošt Kraus and Leda-Lederer died in Terezin. What did Alfred Fuchs feel as he died, was he reconciled or angry with his Catholic God? The collector of social poetry Illový, the mournful humorist Karel Poláček-Butter, the quiet Jaroslav Papoušek – what did they feel? Our questions fly after them upon the wind, never to be answered. All we know for sure is that the honest historian Kamil Krofta was able to die at home here after the country was freed.

The gallows and the execution ground. A hero whose clenched teeth let no name pass, tortured and killed that fateful night, was Vladimir Tůma; he was preceded to the gallows by Josef Fischer, the poet's brother, by the editors König and Kazetka, Vasil Škrach and Vincy Schwarz. Vladislav Vančura – let this last name shine as a symbol and precious memorial for future time, the incarnation of all that Czech literature has lost.

The company of Czech writers paid a terrible bloody price, a
price which demands of us that we close our ranks and remain
true to their memory. Thank you, my friends."

That was a requiem for the dead. And for six long years of darkness.
The words of A. M. Tilschová presenting Jiřina Tůmová need
no commentary; her right to report on the work of the Czech
Club was clear, and we give her words in full:

"As requested by the committee, I am including the treasurer's
report in my account of the activities of the Club from the plenary
meeting of June 6, 1939, to April 17, 1942, when the Gestapo
dissolved the Club.

You will remember that our meeting in June 1939 was held
after the German invasion. We had to decide then what to do with
the money in our possession, which was partly the assets of the
Club and partly the money left over after the 1938 Congress. It
was proposed either to set up a study foundation, or to establish
a convalescent home for writers, or to do both if funds were suffi-
cient. The committee was fully aware that the PEN Club, as part
of an international federation, would not be viewed favorably by
our new self-imposed rulers, and it was a question of protecting
our little capital from their rapacious greed. The meeting gave the
committee a free hand to decide the matter to the best of their
ability. There proved to be many difficulties in the way of a foun-
dation, and so it was decided to concentrate on building a conva-
lescent home. A suitable location was found in Budislav, near
Litomyšl, and the best of the sites willingly offered by the Lito-
myšl authorities was chosen. It was a practical choice. Being
close to the main road, electricity could be laid on easily; and the
surroundings were just what tired city dwellers imagined as the
ideal peaceful retreat: on a small grassy hill sloping down to a
trout brook, with a wooded slope rising gently on the other side.
The purchase was finalized and the architect Stanislav Tobek,

whose plans were approved by the committee, was entrusted with the building of the home. To ensure that the PEN Club's intentions would be respected, a secret arrangement was made with the local authorities of Litomyšl, by which they became the owners of the home and those responsible for its upkeep, until the country returned to normality and the PEN Club could resume ownership. All the Club's money, settled in the Živnobanka, and the proceeds of the sale of its investments, were presented to Litomyšl as a gift; this was the sum of 252,404 crowns. As you are aware, of course, the value of the Czech crown fell after the German invasion, prices rose and this sum was not sufficient; seeking financial support we were aided by Dr. Nedvídek of the Ministry of Public Works, who slipped a grant of 120,000 crowns into his budget for 1941, at the last moment. This was of course in the name of the Litomyšl authorities. The Ministry of Education added a grant of 20,000 for the same purpose, and so the building could be completed. The roof was firmly in place; it remained to equip the interior and dig a well. An electric pump had been purchased, as well as ticking and feathers for the bedding. All these things were stored in Litomyšl, safely away from the eyes of our 'protectors.'

We hoped that we could start some activity and thus find the money to completely equip the home, but even an unfinished building attracted the unwelcome attention of the Wehrmacht. However, it had only twenty-two beds, which did not come up to the requirements of German 'magnificence' for comfort. The authorities in Litomyšl, and especially the municipal secretary Biskup, executed later by the Gestapo, willingly and selflessly helped us, although the affair was fraught with danger for them. According to the records carefully kept by Biskup, the cost of building came to 351,624 crowns; the Litomyšl authorities received altogether 392,404 crowns. There remained 40,780 crowns to our credit as of 13. 2. 1942.

I would like to add that since we have not the means to finish the home ourselves, it would perhaps be wise to turn to the Litomyšl authorities, i. e. the local National Committee, asking them to carry on , and hand the building over to us when completed. In view of all that Litomyšl has always done for us and writers generally, I have no doubt we could come to some agreement. It is for the plenary meeting, of course, to decide. Biskup's account, written before his execution, brings us to the year 1942. As you know, we tried to carry on, although severely limited under the Germans, holding a plenary meeting in 1940 and one in 1941, and dealing with official business mainly concerning our statutes. As you know, the name Czechoslovakia, that evil kingdom, had to be removed. The Club could not arrange any events because no public activity was permitted in the vast concentration camp that our country had become. Yet we did not want to disappear voluntarily, nor did we imagine breaking up the Club. The committee continued to meet in the homes of its members, doing its best to fulfill the main task entrusted to it by the last plenary meeting: to finish the convalescent home and ensure its functioning. We knew things were not going to be easy, and one task we decided to undertake was to hide the Club's papers. Those dealing with the Congress had already been taken to safety in the National Museum; the rest, concerning Club life, were buried in metal boxes in the garden of the house of K. J. Beneš, our vicechairman, in Rožmitál. I would like to thank him publicly, here. Working as he was for the Resistance, Dr. Beneš had plenty to hide, yet he did not hesitate to take this risk. When we learned of his arrest we were distressed for many reasons, not least because of the illegal hoard buried in his garden. To hide the lack of Club records the plenary meeting had passed a resolution offering them for the recycling campaign which had just been announced with great fanfares of patriotic publicity, and this had been made public. If the Gestapo found the Club papers really existed, and that they were buried in his garden, Beneš would have been in very great danger. Fortunately we were dealing with forces that for all their merciless brutality were extraordinarily stupid. They did not search the garden, and Beneš was spared aggravating evidence against him.

The clouds that began gathering round the PEN Club in 1941 only thickened in 1942, and we hesitated to call a plenary meeting for fear of attracting unwelcome attention. As an excuse we had the slight injury A. M. Tilschová had incurred. Shortly after April 10th there was a broadcast lecture on the anti-Nazi attitudes of various Jewish-Freemason and other alien institutions, and the PEN Club was one of those named. I did not hear the talk myself, since for obvious reasons we had no radio at home, but since I was responsible for keeping Club members informed, I was told at once, and was able to get rid of compromising papers. We waited to see what would happen next, and indeed a few days later A. M. Tilschová was called to the Gestapo, on April 17th. We had agreed beforehand what our story would be, so that nobody but she and I would be involved. We presented the PEN Club as an innocent ladies-only society that was only there to provide hospitality – something women were best fitted to do, and so on. It was certainly a great advantage for us that the Club was chaired by a dignified lady who spoke perfect German, and was completely in command of the situation. After the Germans had interviewed her (and accompanied her right to her apartment, certainly not just out of politeness) it was my turn. The Gestapo officer was furious when he heard that we had no records except the essential minutes and a list of members (naturally doctored). He had to be satisfied with the recorded resolution of the 1941 plenary meeting, stating in black and white that unnecessary PEN Club papers should be handed over for recycling. My apartment was searched – which cost me 10,000 crowns worth of books stolen – but nothing incriminating about the Club was found. The Gestapo confiscated those Club records that had been cooked up for them. Alas, copies of those papers, carefully hidden from the Gestapo, were stolen when my apartment was robbed in February of that year. The Germans also confiscated the "wealth" of the Club, consisting of 478 crowns 95 hellers in a Post Office savings book, and about 2,000 crowns in the Dejvice Savings Bank. The committee had deliberately left these sums visible, since it would have made matters much worse if the Germans could find nothing to steal. They could not confiscate the convalescent home because it was to all intents and purposes the property of the municipality of Litomyšl.

The two of us were called to the Gestapo on two more occasions, A. M. Tilschová to bring in the Dejvice savings book, and myself to bring in the confiscated material and the books of mine that were stolen from me. The third occasion was a purely formal one,

when we were informed that as of April 17th the Club was dis-
banded, and made to sign copies of our interrogations. These in-
terviews were certainly very unpleasant and cost our chairwoman
much nervous stress and many tranquilizers, but we achieved
what we set out to do – to save the other members of the Club,
especially the men, many of whom were involved with the resist-
ance movement; interrogation about apparently innocent activity
could sometimes offer the Gestapo clues to far more dangerous
things. I am sure that I speak for all of you in thanking A. M.
Tilschová for her skill and courage in taking on herself this un-
pleasant and dangerous task. Soon after the Germans entered
Prague the Gestapo called Professor R. J. Marek, one of our mem-
bers, and interrogated him on the financial affairs of the PEN
Club, asking particularly about funds from abroad. He replied
firmly that Czech writers had never taken foreign money, and
seeing that there was no wealth to be gained there, the unselfish
invader left us alone. The less than three thousand crowns they
confiscated in 1942 exhausted their interest in us, and the exist-
ence of the PEN Club in the Protectorate was brought to an end.

As you are aware, however, our members in exile in England
set up the Czechoslovak PEN Club in London, presided over by
our beloved František Langer. It came into being in 1940 and
exerted great energy; its laudable activities strengthened our ties
with our English friends. The secretary of the London PEN Club,
Viktor Fischl, is present and after I have finished will present his
report on the Czechoslovak PEN Club in London. You will hear
from him all what our members succeeded in doing abroad. They
were our members, Czech writers, and we can record what they
did to the credit of the PEN Club. They spoke when we were
forced to keep silent.

You have heard an account of what we did under the Protector-
ate, activities which were known at least to the committee mem-
bers. I must now render an account of another form of activity
carried on for the PEN Club, but in secret. Allow me to go back to
the days of Munich. It was clear to all of us then that Munich was
but the beginning and that there was much worse to come. Many
of our members were in danger for political and racial reasons,
and so my husband and I began to prepare contacts abroad and

ways of communicating with them. We made use of all our per-
sonal friends and contacts, especially with the English and
French PEN Clubs. In England there was our valued friend
Storm Jameson, chairwoman of the London Club, who is here
with us today, and secretary Herman Ould. In France there was
our wonderful Benjamin Cremiéux, who alas is no longer with
us. You may remember that the English, most of all, felt deep
shame for what had happened, and the English PEN Club
promptly offered us a considerable sum to help those of our mem-
bers who were in danger. We firmly refused, but asked them for
moral support. Our English friends promised to secure British
visas and permits, while Benjamin Cremiéux promised the same
for France. They all kept their promise. The director of the Insti-
tut Français in Prague, Professor Alfred Fichelle, gave us his
willing help and was our contact; we received news and sent ours
back through him, and visas, too. Later we received very effective
help from the Rev. Waitstill Sharp, who was in Prague as the rep-
resentative of American Relief for Czechoslovakia. He took Pro-
fessor J. B. Kozák back with him, and helped in other cases, too.
March 15, 1939, proved that our preparations had not been wast-
ed. Ways and means had been arranged in good time and many
of those threatened were able to take refuge abroad. Some of the
more sensible had already left before that date. I must confess
that most of the French visas were not used, because some people
refused to leave although they were in danger; I was fearful for
them, but at the same time rejoiced in their courageous attitude.
Some left it too late and then had to escape secretly, over the
Polish border. All those who reached France and especially Eng-
land will tell you how helpful our foreign friends were; our PEN
Club and especially the Prague Congress in the fateful year 1938
proved their importance. It was then that many real friendships
were made, and our friends' knowledge of our life and our coun-
try made them all the more ready to help us. I want to add that
although – at least in the beginning – this was a PEN Club activ-
ity, it did not endanger any of our members here. I need not tell
you that I would never allow anyone else to bear the consequences
of my own actions. I hope and believe that you will give your
approval to what we did, which went to help our Czech people

and did no harm to the Club's reputation, quite the contrary. The PEN Club can be proud of its record. It did not break up, but was dissolved from above. It saved all that could be saved, including human lives. It signed no shameful declarations and showed no 'patriotic' cowardice. You have heard the names of those who were sacrificed. That is one more proof of the courage of those who lived and worked among us.

Allow me one more remark in conclusion. In 1938 when we were preparing the Congress, the committee considered plans to gain the support of Russian writers for the PEN Club idea. Alas, the invasion of Austria and what followed, which influenced the Congress itself as well, made this impossible. During the Congress the matter was discussed with H. G. Wells, and as our ambassador Prokop Maxa will confirm, at dinner with members of the committee Wells heartily approved our plan. He often returned to the idea during the war, and as I have learned from our members who spent those years in England, relations between them and those Russian writers who visited England were very cordial. It would certainly be a good thing if the renewed activity of our Club included this good intention and we could put our plan into practice. Please give the matter your consideration. The international quality of the PEN organization is not divisive, but aims at uniting writers from all over the world in the fight against what we may call fascism, and Russian writers should therefore be engaged with us. Prague enjoys the attention of Russian writers these days, and we shall certainly have the opportunity of welcoming them to the Club.

Before you decide to approve the report of the Club's activities, please remember all those who helped us, at home and abroad, and particularly the English and the French PEN Clubs. We can only thank our dear friend Benjamin Cremiéux in our hearts, but we have Storm Jameson here with us. If you agree, I will thank her in your name."

The two years which followed this plenary meeting of the regenerated PEN Club saw developments in Czechoslovakia which differed considerably from those elsewhere in Central and Eastern Europe. The Writers' Congress organized in Prague ten years after that of the Slovak writers in Trenčianské Teplice was still held in the spirit of anti-fascist unity and tolerance. The new spirit expressed in the congress slogan "The Individual and the Collective" was taken to mean democratic intellectual discussion by the three speakers concerned, two individualists, one a Catholic, and one Marxist. This "settling of accounts and new prospects," as the Congress was called, was not a return to the sharp disagreements between the left and the liberal writers and their Catholic colleagues, characteristic of the pre-war years. Now the emphasis was on the future, and on unity with variety. In the last free elections the battle between the two strongest parties, the National Socialists and the Communists, was won by the latter, yet for the most part Czech Communist intellectuals took their own stand. In September 1946, for instance, they absolutely refused to condone Ždanov's anathema against Zoščenko and Achmatová, and their reaction to the exhibition of Soviet art of the school of socialist realism was reserved if not ironic. On some important issues they had the support of well-known artists; for instance, in the heated public discussion of the new Theater Law which was against private enterprise in the theater, directors like Honzl, E. F. Burian and Frejka openly spoke for a theater which would be economically and ideologically independent, in the spirit of Vilar, Louis Jouvet, Max Reinhardt and Federico Garcia Lorca. The dogmatic sectarian forces grew ever stronger, however, as the proposed hegemony of the Cultural Community showed. The non-communist intellectuals' rejection of this proposal led to the establishment of a Cultural Union and much bargaining. The non-communist intellectuals had relied on the support of a government minister, Stránský, and the writers and journalists Václav Černý and Ferdinand Peroutka. In the atmosphere of democratic discussion which distinguished Czechoslovakia from the other countries of post-war Central Europe with their officially decreed unity, ideas were accepted by force of argument and agreed to, not forced upon the public from above. That all ended in February 1948.

We have already explained that by presidential decree all organizations dissolved by the Nazis were able to start up again in

1945, and the PEN Club did so, announcing the fact to the four ministries concerned: Interior, Education, Information and Foreign Affairs. In each case we asked for a grant of 50,000 crowns. The plenary session asked the President of the Republic, Dr. Edward Beneš, to be the Club' s honorary chairman, and honorary membership was offered to Petr Bezruč, Jaroslav Kvapil, S. K. Neumann, Ivan Olbracht, Albert Pražák, Fráňa Šrámek and Karel Toman. With the exception of S. K. Neumann they all accepted and expressed their thanks.

The new committee elected at this meeting consisted of A. M. Tilschová as chairwoman, F. Langer as vice-chairman, J. Kopta as secretary, J. Hrdinová as treasurer and J. Tůmová as assistant secretary. The remaining members were K. J. Beneš, V. Černý, F. Halas, E. Konrád, K. Krejčí, M. Majerová, M. Pujmanová and V. Řezáč.

The first meeting of the Club was held on January 30, 1947, in the National Club on Příkopy, and the guests of honor were Edwin and Willa Muir. The President of the Republic donated 50,000 crowns for the Club's activities, the Ministry of Education 30,000 crowns, and the Ministry of Foreign Affairs 10,000 crowns. And so our regular meetings began with talks by Professor Odložilík and Jiří Mucha, on February 27th, describing how writers worked in exile. It was far from our minds that the subject would once again become topical.

At the International PEN Congress in Sweden the vice-chairman of the Czech Club, František Langer, spoke of the resistance to the Nazis put up by Czech writers. He headed a delegation of Černý, Hoffmeister, Kopta, Němeček, Papoušková and Tůmová.

In May a lunch was given for Béla Balász; in August the PEN guest was Henri Membre, and in September M. Andersen Nexö. The year was rich in lectures: A. Hoffmeister talked about America on March 27th, V. Borek about the Soviet Union's war on April 24th, Václav Černý about the French Resistance as mirrored in poetry on May 29th, when the editor-in-chief of *Le Soir* was present. On June 26th V. Lacina spoke about cultural life during the Protectorate, our ambassador V. Vaněk talked about the Scandinavian countries during the war on September 25th,

and on October 30th J. Dolanský spoke about the Gate to Freedom of Yugoslavia. The subject of literature and the resistance
movement was touched on again the following year, when Karel
Krejčí talked about Polish poets and the war. The atmosphere of
the war years was still felt in the several attempts made to get
Soviet writers to join the PEN Club, naive as these efforts may
have been. The Czech Club wrote a letter to the Union of Soviet
Writers, to be delivered by the hand of Jarmila Glazarová, at
that time our Cultural Attaché in Moscow. Our initiative was
supported by a letter from the French section of the Belgian
PEN Club. The chairman of International PEN, H. G. Wells, had
long urged Soviet writers to join. In 1949 the London executive
committee was still urging Soviet writers to join. Two of them,
Simonov and Fadějev, arrived, but declared that since there
were fifteen thousand writers in the USSR, there would be no
room for anybody else if they joined. Another reason why they
could not join was that the PEN Club was a nonpolitical organization, while it was the duty of Soviet writers to be political.

The revival of international contacts was attested by the Zurich Internationl PEN Congress in the first week of June 1947,
attended by A. M. Tilschová at the head of the Prague delegation
of Jirko, Konrád, Kopta, Krejčí, Langer and Tůmová. At the end
of June a letter announced that the Bulgarian PEN Club, dissolved by the Nazis as ours had been, was again active, led by
the poet Dora Gabe, well-known in Prague, Ludmil Stojanov and
Kamen Zidarov. In September Lacham of the Chilean Club arrived in Prague, followed by Herman Ould, an important figure
in the London executive of International PEN, who had not been
in Prague since the 1938 Congress.

Things looked as if they were as normal as in pre-war days;
the Czech Club went ahead with an ambitious lecture program
inaugurated by František Langer at the end of January, talking
about Czech poet Fráňa Šrámek. After Krejčí's talk about Polish
poets and the war, Professor Jan Rypka gave a lecture at the end
of March on Iran at the center of world politics. On March 30th
Professor V. Příhoda opened a topical discussion on the single
school system, on June 22nd the Zurich delegation gave an account of the Congress, and on June 1st Karel Nový and Jiří Pis-

torius spoke of Vladislav Vančura as a writer and as a human being, honoring the anniversary of his death as a martyr. The growing political tension does not seem to have affected the PEN Club as yet. The committee met for the first time that year on January 13th, and agreed to celebrate Karel Čapek on the 28th. J. B. Čapek would discuss his writings and František Langer would talk about the human side. Eddmond Konrád would speak on the sixtieth birthday of František Langer, February 25th. The first of these two events took place, and Langer delighted his audience with the "Lesser Talents of Karel Čapek." We learned how Čapek the amateur photographer made the same deliberate mistakes as Čapek the student of English, followed his draughtsmanship through many an incarnation, and got to know Čapek the collector of folk songs among foreign peoples, Čapek the entomologist and the connoisseur of carpets, and – surprisingly – Čapek the lover and connoisseur of wines. The charming memoir ended with an imitation of Čapek with one over the eight, conceived as a self-portrait. Many years later this essay appeared in the delightful book *Byli a bylo* by Langer (*They Lived and It Happened*).

This delightful evening took place only a month before what historians will probably always call the "events of February." In itself this fact reveals the atmosphere of the Czech PEN Club. Louis Golding was expected to arrive, and Graham Greene, never absent when there was something in the air. And the twenty-fifth of February was the day on which Edmond Konrád should have talked about František Langer, now sixty.

Such were the Club's plans, which certainly did not envisage the setting up of an Action Committee to carry out a purge of its members and officers, as all institutions in Czechoslovakia were then forced to do.

The Action Committee of the PEN Club was made up of M. Fábera, A. Hoffmeister, J. Kopecký, V. Lacina and J. Tůmová. It met on March 8th without Fabera and Hoffmeister, who sent their excuses. According to the minutes: "The members of the Action Committee considered the list of members and altered it according to the guidelines laid down by the Syndicate of Czech Writers. The following were considered unfit to be members:

Ivan Jelínek, A. C. Nor and Ferdinand Peroutka. Julius Firt and Petr Zenkl were also crossed off the list of members. A. C. Nor relinquishes his function of accountant and is replaced by Miloslav Faber. The Action Committee agreed that the Club would be represented on the international executive committee in London by Arnošt Vaněček, who was to leave for England as the guest of the British Council. J. Tůmová, originally delegated by the committee, was unable to undertake the journey for reasons of health and other engagements." Ten days later the Czech PEN Club informed the Central Action Committee of the National Front, in Valentinská Street, of the names of the members of its committee for 1948. In order of rank the officers were A. M. Tilschová, F. Langer, J. Kopta, J. Hrdinová and J. Tůmová, with ordinary members M. Majerová, M. Novákova, V. Černý, F. Halas, A. Hoffmeister, M. Jirko, K. Krejčí, J. Mucha, with F. M. Čebiš and M. Fábera as stand-ins.

An extraordinary general meeting was called for April 28th, but the main matter to be discussed was far from political: it was the future of the Budislav convalescent home. As Jiřina Tůmová had reported at the first general meeting in November 1945, the Prague Club had decided to save the Club's funds after the German invasion by investing them in the building of a convalescent home for writers. In 1939–40 the Club thus invested 226,855 crowns and bonds for a value of 29,000. That was a considerable sum of money at the time. It is worth mentioning that further aid was provided from government funds, 120,000 crowns by the Ministry of Public Works, 20,000 by the Ministry of Education, and another 20,000 crowns by the Ministry of the Interior in 1943. After the war the PEN Club received a further 170,000 crowns from various sources. Bills paid in cash amounted to 87,626 crowns, so that the Club could say that 673,461 crowns had been invested in the Budislav home. It was proposed that the home should be handed over to the Syndicate of Czech Writers, but objections were raised that the Syndicate already had the Dobříš manor, which was enough for its needs. The representative of the Syndicate, Dr. Karel Scheinpflug, decided that both places could be well used, Dobříš for prestigious occasions and Budislav for writers to work and rest in. The meeting then agreed to hand the convalescent home over to the Syndicate for the use of writers and their guests.

There is no record of the PEN Club appearing in public after this "Budislav" meeting, but the committee continued to meet, and in the minutes for September 23rd we find that "Dr. Langer suggested that it would be wise to find out whether the future existence of the PEN Club was politically desirable. Jiřina Tůmová was asked to discuss this with the Ministry of Information and take steps accordingly. In any case it was essential to begin preparations for this year's general meeting."

The plenary session was prepared, and took place on December 14th 1948. A month earlier the Club had celebrated the seventy-fifth birthday of the chairwoman, A. M. Tilschová, with a talk by Professor Karel Krejčí, under the aegis of two ministers "for culture," Z. Nejedlý and V. Kopecký.

The general meeting was told that A. M. Tilschová would become honorary chairwoman while her place would be taken by Marie Majerová, who was then sixty-six. There were other changes: Václav Lacina was to take the place of František Langer, while Josef Kopta remained secretary, J. Hrdinová treasurer, and J. Tůmová administrative secretary. Those present at this general meeting were J. Weil, A. M. Tilschová, Z. Horová, M. Stehlík, Z. Hoffmanová, M. Calma-Veselá, F. Kafka, E. Konrád, M. Prušáková, J. R. Marek, V. Vaněk, V. Příhoda, Melniková-Papoušková and J. Tůmová.

From its foundation in 1925 up to the fifteenth of March 1939, the PEN Club was the organizer of what came to be known after 1945 as "cultural contacts with foreign countries." In the times of Čapek this meant writers of different countries meeting each other, with no more political goals than to be nonpolitical. In those days the PEN Club had the monopoly on international contacts between writers, because the Czech Writers Syndicate was not interested, and the other small groups (Svatobor, Blok, Kolo moravskych spisovatelů and others) had not the opportunity. Thus the PEN Club's list of guests and excursions during the fourteen years of its existence gives a practically complete picture of the international contacts of Czechoslovak writers.

Things were different after 1945. Leading intellectuals were given positions in the newly formed Ministry of Information (Bauer, F. Halas, L. Linhart, M. Majerová, V. Nezval, B. Novák, I. Olbracht, J. Zieris and others), and a special department was set up for cultural contacts with abroad, led until the summer of 1948 by the last elected chairman of the Czech PEN Club, Adolf Hoffmeister. This department was organized geographically, and the people in charge were true experts, Jilovská, Hilská, Navrátil, Hrdlička, Fučík, Málek, Polák, Kukla. Well-known people were then sent to serve as cultural attachés in Czechoslovak embassies abroad: Milada Součková and František Vrba to the US, Jarmila Glazarová and Peter Jilemnický to the USSR, Ivo Fleischmann to Paris, Aloys Skoumal to London, Peter Karvaš to Bucharest, Jaroslav Fučík to Rome, Jiří Meisner to Belgrade, Norbert Frýd to Mexico and so on.

The Union of Czechoslovak Writers, formed on the model of the Soviet Writers Union as an "ideological organization" in 1949, soon created its own foreign department (Schwarzová, Stříbrná, Svozilová, Kupka, Maršíček, Pujman).

The fact that the Ministry of Information had a department dealing with cultural contacts abroad meant that all groups, and that also included the PEN Club, were subordinated to it. At first, up to February 1948, things worked, because the department was full of initiative, dynamic and anxious to maintain good contacts with the well-established foreign cultural institutions working in Prague, such as the Institut Ernest Denis, the British Council, the Scandinavian Society and others.

After February 1948 things changed abruptly. Communist Party organs and the Ministry of Foreign Affairs began a purge of these institutions, but not, of course, those dealing with cultural relations with the Soviet Union. Official guarantees of the right behavior were of course required of our colleagues in other People's Democracies (Poland, Yugoslavia, etc.).

Thus the cultural sphere which had been free ground for the PEN Club monopoly became a place governed by regulations, dependent and closely followed. The PEN Club could only note this and take what decisions seemed viable.

If we describe the six years between Munich in 1938 and May of 1945 as a cruel episode during which the PEN Club did not exist and its members were either in exile or were persecuted and executed at home, then the years between 1945 and 1947 could be seen as a time to get one's breath before the "events" of February 1948. This stage in the life of the PEN Club, ending with the "great April plenary session" of 1969, is something new and unaccustomed in our history. It seems impossible to find the right description for this phase, which on closer examination seems to divide into two phases. A metaphor will offer the best answer: *Yes and No, or The Cage in a Bird,* the Czech translation of the book by the French writer Ribemont-Dessaignes. Perhaps the best description of this phase in the history of the Czech PEN Club, antagonism within the Club and within the members themselves.

As the year 1949 opened, the PEN Club was determined to carry on in its traditional manner, and arranged a lecture for the end of January: "Greece's Problem Today, In Light of History," given by S. Maximos. For the 6th of April the Israeli Counselor Uriel Felix Doron was invited to talk about Palestine and the State of Israel. Neither of these lectures incurred the displeasure of the post-February regime.

The Club did not attend the international congress in Venice that year, as the matter could not be negotiated with the Ministry in time. The committee met three times during the year, with Čebiš, Krejčí, Langer, Vaněček and Tůmová present on the first occasion, the absent Hrdinová, Kopta and Nováková excused. The second meeting was attended by Čebiš, Krejčí, Lacina, Nováková, Vaněček and Tůmová, with Kopta and Langer excused. At the third meeting, those present were the same; Kopta asked to be relieved of his function on the grounds of poor health. Our devoted colleague Mrs. Hrdinová died. The plenary meeting was the fifth since 1945, and the twentieth all told. It agreed to allow A. M. Tilschová to give up the office of chairwoman she had selflessly filled for so long and become honorary chairwoman. Her place was taken by M. Majerová. Kopta was succeeded as secretary by Sekera, with Lacina as vice-chairman,

Čebiš as treasurer and Tůmová as permanent administrative secretary. The remaining members of the committee were Kopta, Krejčí, Langer, Nováková, Pujmanová, Vaněček and Závada, with Fáber and Urbánková as stand-ins. Although the Communist Party was now more strongly represented, those concerned were not of the rabid variety. That certain names were still in evidence was a guarantee that the nonpolitical political line followed hitherto would continue to be the Club's policy. If it was to survive, however, the PEN Club would have to be to some extent adaptable.

At the very beginning of 1951 the Czech PEN Club was reminded that it was still an international organization, by a letter from an unexpected source – the German Democratic Republic. Signed by J. R. Becher, B. Brecht, A. Seghers and A. Zweig, it asked the Czech Club to take a stand on the question of a united Germany. This the Club did immediately:

"The Czech PEN Club greets the efforts of democratic German writers to ensure a united, democratic and peace-loving Germany, as set out in the declaration by J. R. Becher, B. Brecht, A. Seghers and A. Zweig, and gives them wholehearted support in this important contribution to world peace. Signed by M. Majerová, A. M. Tilschová, M. Pujmanová, I. Olbracht, V. Řezáč, J. Sekera, V. Lacina, K. Konrád."

At this time the writers of West Germany were also taking this stand and their meeting in Wiesbaden "expressed their determination that literature should serve the unification of Germany and help to ensure world peace." Among the twenty-one writers from West Germany were such well-known names as K. Edschmid, G. Weisenborn, A. von Hatzfeld, Fritz Usinger, Georg von der Wring, Leo Weismantel, Luise Rinser, Ernst Petzold, Ernst Kreuder, M. L. Kaschnitz, Hans Henry Jahn and Erich Kästner. J. R. Becher and S. Hermlin were present from East Germany. The meeting was positively received by both the *Frankfurter Neue Presse* and the *Frankfurter Allgemeine Zeitung*. It was the first time since 1945 that such an event had been organized in West Germany. Arthur Koestler opposed it, however. The Czech PEN Club was preparing to send three delegates to the next International PEN Congress, to be held in Lausanne, but the Ministry of Information did not reply to the Club's letter. No delegates attended, but an apologetic letter was sent instead.

Not many events were arranged at home that year. The theatrical producer Vojta Novák and his wife Milena, a member of the PEN Club committee, talked about the work and life of an actress on February 28th; a month later Arnošt Vaněček gave a lecture on Negro poetry in the United States, and in April the painter F. V. Mokrý talked about Russian and Soviet art.

The general meeting on March 19th of the following year heard this explanation of the Club's poor performance: "The reason why so few lectures were given last year was that the committee of the PEN Club had to spend so much time negotiating with the Ministry of Information for its further activities. These talks went on for some time, but we are happy to inform you that we have found understanding among leading officials and we can carry on. There is hope that our contacts with PEN Clubs in other people's democracies will become more fruitful."

Which people's democracies had a PEN Club? In December that year the Czech committee had met Leon Kruczkowski, who thought the Polish and Czech clubs could co-operate more. There were also clubs in Hungary and in Germany. The archives carry no mention of any activity in Romania or Bulgaria, while Yugoslavia was on the other side of the barricades, farther away than London or Paris.

The fact that both the Ministry of Information and the Ministry of Foreign Affairs were benevolently inclined towards the PEN Club was not to be taken lightly at that time; the chairman of the Club, Arnošt Vaněček, who had succeeded M. Majerová, reported that the Union of Writers (represented by V. Pekárek) was not in favor of the Club. Fortunately the Union was not the final authority and the Ministry of Information asked the PEN Club to submit its report and its plans for the coming year.

After the general meeting Vaněček again headed the committee, with Sekera as secretary and Nováková as treasurer. Mařánek replaced Lacina as vice-chairman. The Ministry of Information, which was the Club's overseer, did not want changes in the leadership, but was interested in gaining new members and in sending a delegation to the International PEN Congress in Nice.

A telegram to Nice announced three delegates (Majerová, Nezval, Branislav) and because the last-named was not a member of the PEN Club, that had to be rectified at once. The necessary official steps were so slow, however, that in the end an apologetic telegram arrived in Nice instead of a delegation.

In September the Ministry of Information was interested in the proceedings of the Nice Congress, but a letter to the London Center was referred to the next issue of *PEN News*. Thus one misunderstanding (if this is the right word) led to another. The PEN bird with its cage within had to wait a long time to be freed. All the more so since 1952 was the year when death sentences from the Prague trials were carried out in the very heart of the leading political force. The atmosphere in Prague in the autumn of 1952 can best be portrayed by the minutes of the PEN Club committee meeting on October 2nd:

"... We proceed to the delicate matters which necessitated this meeting. The Club has received a political publication from England which must be passed on to our superior organ at once. The organ in question, according to the Committee, is the fourth section of the Ministry of Information, to whom the paper will be sent. It could not be sent earlier because the chairman and other responsible members of the committee were not in Prague. For the time being the publication was secured in a sealed envelope and placed in an inaccessible place and locked away. The chairman confirmed that the envelope had not been opened when it was taken from this place; it was placed in another envelope, sealed and signed by the chairman. The secretary of the Czech PEN Club sent the letter to the Ministry, signed by the chairman and vice-chairman of the Club, in an envelope marked 'Confidential.' The signatures are appended."

This official account reminds one of the Chartreuse de Parme, and may evoke smiles today, but we should remember that a few weeks later the trial of the "treacherous spies" was to take place, and that one of the outstanding members of the PEN Club was Jiřina Tůmová, who had so courageously and wisely represented

the PEN Club before the Gestapo. It is convincing evidence of
that time when "no hope was a way of life," for the principal
authority was fear. This must be borne in mind when seeking
the right angle from which to view the Czech Club's activities:
May 14th, Bohumil Polan spoke about Karel Toman; on October
5th, Jaroslav Závada spoke about Petr Bezruč; on November
11th, J. Dolanský spoke about N. V. Gogol, and on December
10th, F. V. Mokrý lectured on Mikuláš Aleš. Pavel Eisner, Edmond Konrád, N. Melniková-Papoušková and Professor Václav
Příhoda were among the audience.

This was the year when Milada Horáková and Záviš Kalandra were sentenced and executed in Prague. André Breton wrote
an open letter to Paul Eluard, but in vain; Eluard did not inter-
vene on Kalandra's behalf. That these attitudes existed among
the avant-garde in the west, the Czechs were not allowed to
know until many years later.

That was the atmosphere at the turn of that fatal year which
hung over the PEN Club like a threatening disease. PEN was at
fault by the very fact that it existed – an existence which called
for never-ending demarches and negotiations with the authorities. The committee wrote repeatedly to the Ministry of the Interior, the Ministry of Information, and the Central Committee
of the Communist Party, and as the regime grew ever fonder of
reorganization there emerged a new organ "modelled" on the
Soviet Union, the Commission for Cultural Relations with Foreign Countries. This body took over the functions of the Fourth
Department of the Ministry of Information, and bureaucracy
became ever more complicated. The chairman Vaněček, the secretary Sekera and Jiřina Tůmová spent a great deal of time in
March 1953 knocking at the doors of officialdom. Dr. Oldřich
John, chairman of the Central Action Committee of the National
Front, was asked to help speed up official recognition of the PEN
Club's statutes. At about this time the Club was in danger of
losing its only meeting-place, as half of Jiřina Tůmová's apartment was allotted to a second tenant. The reform of the Czechoslovak currency presented another threat, because unless the
Club's statutes were officially recognized and registered as a
member of the National Front, its funds would be changed at the

rate for private individuals (1 : 50) instead of 1 : 5, and that would be a catastrophe.

Similar forces to those undermining the Czech PEN Club at home were criticizing it abroad for not being active enough. The chairman of the German Ost und West PEN Club, J. Trolow, demanded that the Czech Club attend the International Congress in Amsterdam and thus strengthen the fight for peace. The Czechs were to attend a meeting of the Executive Committee in Dublin, but were prevented because the Union of Writers insisted on its own two delegates, neither of whom spoke English, although the PEN Club candidate not only spoke the language but knew Ireland well...

Despite this atmosphere of absurdity the Czech PEN Club went on with its program of lectures: on January 20th, a very successful one by Albert Pražák on Vrchlický; in April, F. V. Mokrý on the painter Jaroslav Čermák; A. M. Píša on Jiří Wolker; on May 27th V. Tichý on Žofie Podlipská; in November K. Polák on Tereza Nováková. As we see, the classics offer the same safe harbor in the icy waters of Stalinism as under the Nazi occupation.

In March both Stalin and Gottwald were relieved of their duty to fight for peace and passed to the peace of eternity, but much time would have to pass before the thaw could set in.

No wonder that the PEN Club was entirely taken up with the struggle for survival. A committee meeting on October 1, 1953, was told by the chairman Arnošt Vaněček that "since both the Central Committee of the Communist Party and the Central Committee of the National Front had given their approval, the responsible official of the Ministry of Culture was asked to meet the chairman and secretary of the PEN Club in the offices of the Writers' Union. He was informed that the legalization of the PEN Club needed to be speeded up for many reasons, one of which was the question of ensuring that the Club's funds would be allowed the exchange rate of 1 : 5 by the State Bank. It was urgent that official recognition be granted quickly."

So much for that committee meeting. The Club continued to exist somehow, while the reorganization fever saw the disappearance of ministries (including Information) and state commissions (including that for cultural relations with foreign countries).

Nothing changed with the advent of 1954, and the minutes of the committee meeting of January 20th again record that it was urgent to ensure the Club's continued existence, now under the authority of the Ministry of Culture, and the secretary promised to ask for an interview with the deputy minister. The next committee meeting two months later learned that things had not moved forward because the Minister was in Poland.

There is no record of whether things moved forward after the Minister got back from Poland, but the fact that on May 26th, M. Nováková lectured on Božena Němcová means that the Club still lived. It was not until June 10th that the secretary (Sekera) had two positive things to report: it had been decided in principle that delegates would be sent to the Amsterdam Congress. And the Club was allowed to go on existing. We learn from the minutes of the committee meeting on September 23rd that articles on the Amsterdam Congress appeared in the press, written by František Kubka and Jiří Marek, which well illustrates the influence exerted by the Union of Writers, for the two concerned were sent by the Union, rather than by the PEN Club. Our committee, consisting at that time of Honzíková, Nováková, Tůmová, Krejčí, Mařánek and Skoumal, under their chairman Vaněček, could not expect to put forward any individual policy, but we must admire the persistence (and selflessness) with which they worked for the recognition and very existence of the PEN Club. Unfortunately Sekera, who as secretary was most in contact with officialdom during this time, left no record of the tricks he had to use, nor of those used against him. This was the reign of absolute absurdity, as can be seen from the minutes of the PEN committee meeting of March 6, of the year before:

"J. Tůmová reported that when the announcement of the next general meeting was delivered to the local authority, the messenger was given a circular from the Central Prague Municipal Authority, concerning the new arrangements for clubs in Czechoslovakia. The messenger was further informed that by March 21st the PEN Club must either amalgamate with an existing mass organization, or dissolve itself."

The committee members immediately set in motion the roundabout of intervention with the relevant Ministry, telephoning, writing, putting forward statements of policy, and after a week's activity were informed that the general meeting would be allowed to take place and that there would be no change in the status of the PEN Club.

We have left this piece of earlier history for the moment when we look forward to the next year. In February the PEN Club would celebrate the thirtieth anniversary of its founding as a club for writers to get to know each other and especially to get to know colleagues abroad.

It looks as though from February 1948 onwards the PEN Club was just about alive, concerned primarily to go on living in the weeks ahead. Such a summary dismissal of the Club's activity would be grossly unfair. The committee needed a great deal of stamina not to give in, to refuse ever new waves of negation, to dare to hope in a hopeless situation. It was not their fault; every society has its culture, and if society is sick, so is its culture.

At the end of the second world war a new concept emerged, never thought of before: cultural policy. In fact this meant that politics would rule culture. This concept was welcomed at once, and then one could only speak of a better or worse cultural policy. A totalitarian regime sees itself as the incarnation of the only correct policy; it cannot conceive of any other cultural policy than its own. As this concept was realized from about 1949 onwards, culture was flooded with ideology and lost the ability to develop naturally. Governed by the "demon of consent," culture *a priori* rejected any ideas that were not "ideologically acceptable." Culture no longer sponsored open, public search, no longer put questions, but simply accepted the given answers. This was not an immediate change, nor a simple one, but a struggle between political power and the power of the mind, although the opposition was not always obvious. Power could not live without ideas, pioneer thinking, questions, but it left these matters to its own officials, who were in its hands.

It took a good eight years before culture, that is to say those responsible for culture, came out openly to declare that power and culture were two antagonistic principles. This could only have happened in that sphere where the word, as the instrument of the mind, is supreme: in literature. The Congress of Czechoslovak Writers held in 1956 was the first hostile encounter between culture and politics. And it was not critics or literary theorists, but lyric poets who entered this taboo arena. Jaroslav Seifert and František Hrubín put forward freedom as the fundamental prerequisite for creativity – and for life. This called into question the "ideological direction" of culture, as a contradiction in terms.

Future developments would show how such action could free culture itself. It also showed how illusory was the "nonpolitical" stand of the PEN Club in times so politically tense. This was said in 1938 by Edmond Konrád in his article "The Political History of the PEN Club." The apolitical PEN Club soon began to fulfill its mission, penetrating across political frontiers. A certain degree of freedom, of course, was essential before this could be attempted; just so much freedom, but not less.

It so happened that in November 1956 Dominik Tatarka applied for membership in the Czech PEN Club, a Slovak writer who could have applied to the Slovak Club. Tatarka felt at home in Prague already as a young student, but there was a deeper logic behind his action: his book *The Demon of Consent* was just as strong an impulse for liberation as the speeches made by Seifert and Hrubín in Prague, but the Slovak cultural atmosphere was less open to such steps as yet.

The most startling world event of that year, of course, was the speech of Khruschev revealing the murderous conduct of Stalin under the cloak of his plans for a "joyful future."

"To penetrate across political frontiers" was still not a simple matter, however. It was no coincidence that this was the year Hungarian writers raised Petöfi's banner of freedom. They were forced to take to the barricades with it, to face Soviet tanks (sent by that same conflicted Kruschev), and defeated, found themselves in prison, in exile, and the center of endless arguments tossed about to justify the Cold War. The Hungarian authorities tried to steal the Petöfi banner of freedom, with the slogan "He who is not against us is on our side" spread like a fig leaf over the Soviet occupation of their country and their own collaboration. It was not because Stalinism was more liberal after the Hungarian rebellion, but because it was weakened, that Kadar's government was able to free the jailed writers and install a regime which seemed to offer a vestige of intellectual freedom. Eight years later, in 1964, it was this government that allowed International PEN to organize something as yet unheard of: not only were PEN Clubs in all the "imperialist countries" invited to send delegates to the International Conference in Budapest on October 16–17th, but writers in exile were guaranteed that they would be free to go back to their freedom in exile. This was a historic compromise, and so Tábori and Tigrid were able to meet their fellow writers from "home," while proscribed emigrés from the Baltic states could talk to the Soviet observers at the Congress, Simonov and Markov. It was not until nearly twenty years later that a Russian PEN Club was established, after the fall of the Soviet Union.

History is a master of irony, and it was at this Conference with its mood of historic compromise that a delegate from the West German PEN Club, at a reception at the Ministry of Culture, announced the fall of Kruschev and the succession of Brezhnev and Kosygin. Simonov and Markov listened openmouthed, even more astonished than the others, for they had heard and knew even less than anyone else. Thus the Budapest PEN Conference was perhaps the most significant but also the last event of the "thaw," and the signal for the triumphant advance of neo-Stalinism for the next twenty-five years! Nevertheless the program of the Congress, "Tradition and Modernity in Contemporary Literature," was a fitting end to the series that began in Rome in November 1961.

History did not stand still.

On January 31, 1957, the Czech Club sent the Nobel Committee in Stockholm a letter proposing Professor Jaroslav Heyrovský for the Nobel Prize, a real scientist and inventor who was not in fief to any political party.

On March 14th Pavel Eisner lectured on Franz Kafka. In Budapest, Soviet tanks had finished off the last of the thaw, while in Prague the first modest signs were appearing.

At the general meeting on April 30th, the seasoned warriors
K. Krejčí, M. Pujmanová, J. Mařánek, J. Sekera and A. Vaněček
were joined by A. Bernášková, P. Karvaš, J. Marek, J. Mašek,
V. Nezval, J. Otčenášek and J. Pokorný.

On June 18th Anna Marie Tilschová died. She served the
Club faithfully for thirty-two years and together with J. Tůmová
helped to form the Czech Club's individual style. She was a
great lady. Besides the Ministry of Culture, the notice of her
death was signed only by the Writers Union. The PEN Club was
apparently not thought worthy. Originally Professor Průšek, the
well-known orientalist, should have represented Prague at the
XXIX Tokyo International PEN Congress, but as he was unable
to attend, Adolf Hoffmeister was sent; one of the youngest members of the Club, he had been co-opted on to the committee in
November 1957. The international PEN Club scene was constantly racked by the explosive Hungarian question. It was the
Hungarian writers who first brought discussion of the deadly
nature of Stalinism out into the open; it was the Hungarian
writers who spoke most clearly at the Budapest popular demon-
stration on October 23, 1956; it was they who suffered the
cruellest repressive measures after the defeat of the movement
for revival – the two most important writers, Tibor Déry and
Gyula Hay, were sentenced to life imprisonment; it was the
Hungarian writers who emigrated but also who addressed the
world to protest the appearance of the Hungarian question on
the agenda of the General Assembly of UNO.

Today, Hungary considers the events of 1956 as a legitimate
popular uprising, and there is nothing risky about discussing it.
The Soviet tanks are no longer on alert. In 1957, though, it was
called counterrevolution, and the wrong move could provoke a
repeat performance. International PEN and the Clubs in the
lands of Hungary's neighbors were constantly being embroiled
in the maelstrom of this problem.

At the Tokyo Congress the Hungarian PEN Club was threatened with suspension, if not expulsion, and all depended on the
results of investigation on the spot, undertaken by the secretary of the international executive committee, David Carver.
When the vote was taken there were 13 for and 13 against sus-

pension, and it was the French president, André Chamson, who gave the deciding vote and saved the Hungarian Club. He was effectively supported by the Czechoslovak delegate Adolf Hoffmeister. The Hungarian PEN Club harmed its own cause by not attending the Congress or sending a written report to London beforehand.

The situation was no better at the executive committee meeting on March 18, 1958, as Hoffmeister reported: "In view of the indifference shown by the Peoples' Democracies (i. e. their PEN Clubs), there is no point in our pulling other peoples' chestnuts out of the fire. We are in a strong position, respected for the proper conduct of our affairs and for our conciliatory stand, but we weaken that position by intervening on behalf of Clubs who act literally in an impossible manner, especially the Hungarian PEN Club. The exiled writers demanded that the Hungarian Club be called to account (be immediately suspended), but Tábori is too insistent. Of course it is true that the Budapest Club is making a mess of things. They did not answer Carver's questions, they did not send a list of their members, they have not paid their subscription. Nor have they explained why their chairman Belonyi was nominated instead of being elected. They asked for visas too late and did not attend the meeting."

It is worth noting the differences and similarities between the situation in which the various Central European Clubs found themselves. Here it is appropriate to recall the words of Vítězslav Nezval at the end of the general meeting on May 16, 1957, when he became chairman of the Czech PEN Club. According to the record: "He gave a brief sketch of the new committee's program, aiming at making the PEN Club a vital element in our literary life and a bridge for understanding between us and poets and writers in the West. Many members of the PEN Club are writers who have fallen silent, although they could and should be taking the lead in literary life. It is our job to rally them to go on writing. The PEN Club must be an independent body, and although it cooperates with the Writers Union it must be free in every respect. Our ideological stand is clear and convinced, but not dogmatic. We shall stand by it and defend it, but there must be no doubt that we sincerely want to work together with all writers of goodwill, with those in the West as well. We must gain their confidence, and this means primarily that we must be more active in the international sphere. Nezval proposed that as many as possible of the visits by writers from the Peoples Democracies discussed by the general meeting should be realized, and believes that we should propose Prague for the venue of the next International PEN Congress."

According to the minutes Nezval's speech aroused lively discussion. It could perhaps be read as unexpressed criticism of the existing state of the PEN Club and of culture altogether during the fifties, but if so, it came belatedly, just as the *Belated Reportages* by Ladislav Mňačko did indeed come belatedly after Tatarka's *Demon of Consent*.

That year, 1958, was marked by the death of three members: Vítězslav Nezval, Marie Pujmanová, and Pavel Eisner. Marie Pujmanová was active for years, returning to the committee when Nezval was elected, as a sign of hope for better times. Pavel Eisner was not one of those Prague German writers invited by Karel Čapek in March 1925, but he soon joined, and remained with the Club until his death. His lectures were bright moments in the gloomy years of the fifties. A true polyglot, his finest work was devoted to the Czech language, like his *Temple and Shrine*. His reputation increases as time goes on, and his work will not fall into oblivion.

1958 – the time of the thaw was approaching, even in such frozen regions as Hungary. The Hungarian Club, perhaps feeling the need to repair its tattered reputation, decided to award a medal, "Pro litteris hungaricis," for services to Hungarian literature, to foreign writers, among whom were Ján Smrek, E. B. Lukáč and Štefan Beniak.

Towards the end of the year the Czech PEN Club devoted two lectures to former leading members: on 20th November Professor Karel Krejčí lectured about A. M. Tilschová and on December 18th František Langer talked about Karel Čapek. It is often true that one must look back in order to go forward. New names appeared, Bernášková, Gottlieb, Jirotka, Nesvadba; while others departed, Marek, Saudek and the much lamented Arnošt Vaněček, who bore the heaviest burden of keeping the PEN Club afloat in the icy waters of post-February Czechoslovakia. Perhaps it was his gentle and conciliatory nature that fitted him for that task, just as it underlay his writing, his poetic prose and his translations; he was a borderline person such as the PEN Club always attracted. Maybe the most difficult encounters with the authorities were taken over by Josef Sekera, the more energetic and less gentle secretary. It was natural that the committee found room for Adolf Hoffmeister, a writer, caricaturist and all-round personality whose knowledge of languages and diplomacy made him at home anywhere in the world – even in Prague. He became chairman at the general meeting of the Club on June 9, 1960, after being co-opted on to the committee at the end of 1957.

There were a number of lectures in 1959. Their subjects of course reflected the times. January 29th: L. Čivrný spoke about the Cuban poet N. Guillen; February 26th: F. Buriánek on A. Zápotocký as a writer; April 30th: Z. Eis on M. Pujmanová; October 29th: F. Götz on V. Řezáč; while M. Drozda's lecture on contemporary Soviet writing reflected a new and less sycophantic attitude. On December 11th K. Krejčí talked about Julius Slowacki – a Polish subject once more. Polish writers experienced their own "events" in the autumn of 1956, but suffered far less serious consequences than their Hungarian colleagues. On October 30th two well-known PEN Club members from Brazil, Jaime Adoura de Camaro and Professor Fereira, visited the Club in Prague.

The Hungarian problem did not disappear from the international PEN scene too easily, but reached a crisis again at the jubilee 30th Congress in Frankfurt am Main. In 1956 the Hungarian Club had not elected its leadership according to the statutes; they had been nominated, a fact which led to the suspension of the Club. The international executive set up a committee to make recommendations. After studying the matter, this committee recommended that the Hungarian PEN Club be reinstated as a full member, but this was opposed as before by the Hungarian writers in exile, now supported by the Austrian Club as well. After an excited debate the vote was 19 for reinstatement, 9 against, and 9 abstentions, and so the Hungarian Club became a member again, thanks mainly to the chairman André Chamson. Relations among the international PEN Clubs at that stage of the Cold War were so tense, however, that the Hungarian question could flare up again at any moment. The Czechoslovak delegate to the Frankfurt Congress was Eduard Goldstücker, who was active in public life again after serving years of a jail sentence handed down in the "show" Prague trials of the fifties; he angered the international executive by his criticism of social and political life in West Germany, the host country.

It was not until the Rome meeting of autumn 1961 that final reconciliation became possible, after the Hungarian delegate gave satisfactory evidence that there were no longer any writers in prison in his country. At last the official Budapest delegation could sit round the same tavern table as the exiled writers led by Tábori, and the fruit of their reconciliation was such effective joint propagation of Hungarian literature in the West that it could only be envied.

Looking back, it is clear that the life of the Czech PEN Club from 1948 to 1957 was a struggle for survival, when each year's general meeting was to be seen as success. This period was followed by a certain degree of revival from 1957 to 1969, when the quality of the Club's life was something that could now be considered.

Careful analysis could show the Czech PEN Club gradually assuming a greater role internationally, but it would not be realistic to ignore the part played by exiled writers, particularly the Hungarians, after 1956. This was natural, and only after 1968 and the Soviet invasion of Czechoslovakia did the Czech and to some extent the Slovak emigre writers come to the fore.

A remarkable phenomenon appeared in the complementary activities of the Prague Club and the Czech writers in exile, put into words by Pavel Tigrid at an executive committee meeting, when he said that for the first time in twelve years he and the Prague delegate held views that were close to each other.

It was not bad strategy on the part of the exiled writers to appeal to the Congress of Czechoslovak Writers in 1967 to demand the release of their fellow writers still in prison. Although the answer from Prague, that they would deal with the authorities in their own way, can be explained in tactical terms, the fact that they were incapable of "subsuming the views" of their persecuted, silenced and imprisoned fellows was a decided retreat from the stand taken by Jaroslav Seifert in 1956. At this stage of the Cold War it was the deliberate policy on both sides to confuse and mislead, and in this atmosphere it was a great help when some "Western" Clubs, like the French and the Belgian, tried to meet their "Eastern" colleagues halfway. These attempts to free the international executive committee's policy from the vice of the Cold War showed the will to transcend frontiers that Edmond Konrád praised in his 1938 essay on the nonpolitical character of the PEN Club... Yet it was not so understood by the "Eastern" Clubs whose rigid attitudes brought these efforts to nought, as Hoffmeister pointed out in his report on the Tokyo Congress.

Dr. Karel Petráček prepared a lecture on "The Arabs and Their Literature" for the coming PEN Congress in Iran, proof of the Czech PEN Club's prompt reactions and of the reputation of Czech oriental studies. Despite the "thaw," PEN lectures in Prague were of the lighter variety. At the end of November 1962 the versatile K. Krejčí talked about the "Prehistory of the Detective Story," followed in April by J. Škvorecký on the modern detective story. At the end of that year delegates were sent to the executive committee meeting in London, and could report that the thaw continued and must be encouraged.

Three events arranged by International PEN show that things were moving slowly forward; Czech participation in them was welcomed. A round-table discussion of "Translation and Translators" was held from the first to the fourth of November 1961, in Rome, followed two years later by one in Rheims on "Translation and the Theater." Finally, on October 16–17th, a round-table discussion of "Tradition and Modernity in Contemporary Literature" was held in Budapest, the last of the series.

The Czech PEN Club had acknowledged the importance of translation ever since Karel Čapek, himself the author of innovative translations of modern French poetry, took steps to overcome the supercilious attitude of many writers to the value of translation. A center was created to support foreign translators of Czech writing. Other leading PEN figures, Otokar Fischer, Hanuš Jelínek, Václav Tille and Pavel Eisner, maintained in the heart of the Club this double role so rooted in the tradition of Czech literature. It found expression, too, in a number of theoretical studies, culminating after the war in two works by Jiří Levý which were unique. In his *Art of Translation* he formulated a theory of translation as an art of reproduction, basing his views on Prague structuralism. This is a unique approach aroused great interest and appreciation among his PEN Club listeners.

Active in the discussions in Rome were well-known members of International PEN, like Roger Caillois, Robert Goffin, Jean de Beer, Sofia Ernst, Jaroslav Iwaszkiewicz, Paul Tábori, Alberto Moravia and Lewis Galantiere. They brought translation from its marginal position to the center of interest, discussing both the nature of translation itself and the position of the translator. The original ideas of the Hungarians, the Poles and of course the Czechs were to the fore.

At the Rheims meeting Yves Gandon and Donald Watson, among others, praised the seminal view of translation as an art put forward by the Czechs, and their recognition of the translator's double duty: to the author's original and to the cultural background of the target country. A valuable exchange of views between western avant-garde writers like E. Ionescu and East European writers like Jiří Mucha revealed that despite totalitarian governments it is possible for writers to break through with authentic and sincere works. The debates also showed up two different approaches, that of the market and that of literary content. As Jean de Beer said in his summary: "The question of translations is not basically one of agents or fees, but above all it is one of love, communication and brotherhood."

The question of the translator's role and his or her material situation was equally important in the PEN Club's activities in the international sphere. The view put forward by writers from eastern Europe, i. e. that the translator as well as the author should have his or her own rights and royalties, logically led to acknowledgment of the translator as an autonomous creative artist, the equal of the author in all aspects of cultural policy.

The text of the Rome discussion was published by International PEN with Gary, Tábori and Zavalani as editors; the Rheims discussion appeared in the PEN journal, *Arena*, edited by Jean de Beer and Paul Tábori. We have already mentioned the political aspects of the Budapest symposium, the theme itself already calling for discussion: "Tradition et modernite" in French, "Tradition and Innovation" in English. The nature of tradition and the esteem in which it is held in different cultures determined each speaker's approach to the subject. Writers from such vastly different lands as the Ivory Coast, Egypt and Guatemala brought home to all that in its immense variety the world is an unknown entity as yet little explored, forcing writers to seek common words for very different things. As for the Czechs, the "Prague" delegate Čivrný agreed with the exiled Czech writer Tigrid in describing Václav Havel as an example of how the theater of the absurd was acquiring the role of social critic, showing the existence of alienation in a society that claimed to have been formed in the struggle against alienation.

This strange period in the history of the Czech PEN Club was full of paradox and arbitrary about-face, mirroring the conflicting tendencies within the regime itself. This writer's own experience can serve as an example: in 1960 I was chosen to represent the Czech PEN Club at the Brazil Congress, and had prepared a special publication for the occasion. Four days before my departure, when I had already been given an exit visa (a more important document than the passport itself, in those days), flight ticket and credit card, I was told I would not be leaving. Instead someone else was sent, completely unqualified for the occasion, and not even a member of PEN. The day before he left he had no idea he would be going anywhere. Written protests evoked the explanation that the Brazil Congress was too insignificant an affair for such a well-known personality to attend. Yet a year later I was suddenly allowed to go to the Rome meeting.

Intense activity by the Czech Club in the international sphere was thus a very uncertain business, and promises could not be relied on. The authorities played a cat-and-mouse game, without knowing the reasons for their own decisions. Nevertheless the thaw continued, and the writers of Czechoslovakia were not so easily pushed back into the painful passivity of the fifties. The Writers Congress of 1963 reflected a decidedly critical mood, and the two solitary voices of 1956 were echoed, as visitors from International PEN were able to hear for themselves. In April 1963 Klara Hamerich, chairwoman of the Danish Club, visited Prague, followed in June by the French chairman, Jean de Beer, and in May 1963 the international secretary David Carver himself arrived. An important event of October that year was the visit to Prague of John Steinbeck and Edward Albee, who met with writers at the home of Jiřina Tůmová (according to the record those present were A. Bernášková, L. Čivrný, E. Goldstücker, A. Hoffmeister, A. J. Liehm, J. Nesvadba, O. Scheinpflugová, J. Škvorecký, H. Volanská, F. Vrba and the film producer J. Weis). It so happened that K. Simonov and G. Markov were in Prague at the time, and so these two pairs of writers representing the two antagonistic Great Powers were able to meet in the Writers Club. John Steinbeck went on record with these words: "I don't know what your literary activity is, but surely you have the best cooking of any writers' group in the world." This high praise was well earned by Jiřina Tůmová's hospitality, as well as by the official cooks of the Literarní fond. Nothing of the sort came from either of the Russian pens, although the shift from the literary to the culinary "front" could not have come amiss to these emissaries of that Great Power.

The lectures arranged by the Czech Club also began to be more interesting. In November 1963 K. Krejčí talked about Otokar Fischer and in March 1964 about Pavel Eisner, whose loss had left such an unfilled gap. In December 1963 Radoslav Nenadál gave a talk in celebration of the Thackeray centenary; in February 1964 Jaroslav Schejbal discussed the conception of the hero in American literature, and in April Josef Škvorecký chose the right moment for a talk on "How We Used to Fly to the Moon In the Old Days."

František Langer died on August 2, 1965. He had been one of the leading members of the PEN Club since its founding. In 1916, he was captured in Galicia during the first world war and joined the Czechoslovak Legion in Russia, returning home with them after battling through Siberia. An army doctor, he had the

rank of colonel, and during the second world war he was again
an active officer, commanding the medical services of the Czechoslovak Army in England and sharing the honor they earned
for their part in the Battle of Britain. In civilian life he was a
playwright, the author of *Saint Wenceslas, Millions, A Camel
Through the Eye of the Needle, The Conversion of Ferdyš Pištora,
On the Edge of Society* and *The Victors*. His other prose works
include *The Golden Venus, The Iron Wolf, Dreamers and Murder-
ers* and a delightful book of memoirs, *They Lived and it Happened*, which brings to life Langer's brother Jiří, Jaroslav Hašek,
the friends meeting in the Union and the Arco cafés, and of
course Karel and Josef Čapek, with graphic charm. Langer
worked as the dramatic adviser of the Vinohrady theater from
1935. His plays, along with those of the Čapeks and perhaps
those of Konrád, are the finest legacy of the First Republic; they
were innovative in their view of the world and the way they
presented it, unemphatic and natural, informed with human
understanding and a strong social note – and humorous. Their
everyday metaphoric style was something new, as was the language, described by the critic Šalda as "words from the streets,
uncombed and unwashed," which "the poet made the messengers of eternity." Langer showed dogged courage in the troubles
heaped upon him by the regime after 1948, the imprisonment of
his actress daughter Věra, dismissal from the army, and enforced retirement into the background. In February 1958 he
wrote to Marie Majerová: "You write that it is a pity my 'immense dramatic talents' are lying idle. Why are they lying idle?
The playwright needs the live reaction of his audience, actors,
the theater, more than any other writer. Without them he is
worse than idle, he is dead. And I have been banned in my homeland for the last eight years, indeed for almost eighteen, and
that makes me worse than idle. I am not the only one; Konrád,
Scheinpflugová, Kopta, Vančura, Čapek and others are banned
too. Of course it is a loss for the theater, actors, audience and
readers, but above all it is Czech literature's loss. One day, when
the history of that literature is written honestly, it will be recorded not only as a loss, but as a disgrace. Perhaps the historian will note that of the writers who now play the leading role

and are therefore the most responsible, not one has bothered to take any notice of this state of affairs. Not even you, Marie, until it touched you personally."

The critic Josef Träger spoke for the PEN Club at Langer's funeral, but to this day the Czech theatrical world has done nothing to rehabilitate Langer's work, or that of many others. The producer Francois Truffaut once wrote that a book banned is like a book burned. All who have not lost the sense of tragedy will smell the smoke rising from burned books, a flag of smoke waving over the half-century 1939 to 1989.

But man is an insensitive creature, and a cunning one. How much insensitivity he cunningly dresses up in words when he sets out to be admired for his sensitivity! In September 1965 an international symposium was held in Prague, on the subject of "Man Against Destruction," words that recalled the writings and ideas of Karel Čapek. This mark of honor certainly represented a shift in attitude from the one castigated by Čapek's friend Langer in that letter.

In Czech cultural life things were slowly improving, thanks to a wave of criticism from those people later to be called reform communists. Nevertheless there were unexpected complications. The International PEN Congress in New York invited individual Czech writers, without informing the Czech Club, perhaps hoping to speed up the thaw, but it was an unfortunate move; private persons could not get exit permits, and the Club had not been given time to do so.

Meanwhile, in the Moscow of Brezhnev, something was building up that was a nasty reminder of the fifties – the trial of two critical writers, Daniel and Sinyavski. Some PEN Clubs wrote to protest, some did not. The Czech Club was among the latter. The executive committee learned at its meeting on March 28th that the general secretary David Carver was invited to attend the trial, along with Vigorelli of the Comunitate Europea di Scrittori. The invitation was signed by Tvardovsky and Surkov. It transpired that there were differences of opinion between local PEN Clubs. Soon the Czech Club had problems of its own – the writer Jan Beneš was arrested, and their delegate to the Arnhem executive meeting, Jiří Mucha, was in the difficult situation of complete ignorance of the details. The exiled Czech writers added the case of the *Tvář* journal to the agenda as well. This monthly, which grouped young authors round Václav Havel, was attacked by the conservatives in the Writers Union. Hoffmeister explained the affair as a conflict between two generations rather than a political matter, and Pavel Tigrid agreed with him, adding that he supported his Prague friends as he had done for the last twelve years.

Daniel and Sinyavski received heavy sentences at their Moscow trial. There the frosts had returned, while in Prague they doggedly pursued the thaw. The Czech PEN Club did all it could to present a clear image, to correct the blurred effect produced by the struggle to survive from the fifties onwards. In 1960 we began publishing bibliographical lists of Czech and Slovak translations from specific linguistic spheres, usually for some special occasion. The first list was sent to the 31st International PEN Congress in Rio de Janeiro in July 1960; it covered works from Brazil and Portugal, together with Spanish and Latin American writing, from 1945 to 1960. It was produced under the aegis of Lumír Čivrný, member of the PEN Club committee and translator of Spanish poetry, who wrote in his introduction: "A rich and lively literature has nothing to fear from friendly comparison with others. A free literature, informed with human brotherhood, does not underrate such comparison, but rather seeks it. The earth is not shrinking because man can fly in the universe and distances are no longer so great and people are growing closer together. They are growing and the earth grows great with them."

The next list appeared in April 1963 for the 32nd Congress in Iran, and covered the literatures of the Near East. Academic Professor Jan Rypka, Jiří Bečka, Karel Petráček and Josef Blaškovič wrote the introduction. However, the Congress did not take place in Iran, but in Oslo, and Radko Kejzlar prepared a bibliography of "Scandinavian Literatures in Czechoslovakia from 1945 to May 1964." For the French-Czechoslovak Friendship Week in May 1964, the PEN Club published "French Literature in Czechoslovakia from 1945 to January 1964," introduced by Ivo Fleischman who was then Cultural Attaché in Paris;

Adolf Hoffmeister contributed portaits of of five French writers. For the 33rd Congress in Bled in June 1965, "Yugoslav Literature in Czechoslovakia 1945–1964" appeared with an introduction by Oton Berkopec in which he wrote: "The bibliographical lists of Czech translations published over the last hundred and fifty years give credence to the apparently bold claim that there is probably no other people who have followed the development of the literatures of other countries so closely and with such real knowledge as the Czechs". The PEN Club celebrated the seventh centenary of the birth of Dante Alighieri with "Italian Literature in Czechoslovakia 1945–1964," published in 1965. In her introduction M. Mattušová discussed not only Dante and Czech translations of his works, but the history of Czech-Italian cultural relations. Jaroslav Schejbal wrote the introduction to "American Literature in Czechoslovakia 1945–1964" for the International PEN Congress in New York in June. The Club's secretary, Jiřina Tůmová, prepared all these issues for publication; each was equipped with reliable biographical detail by Zdenka Broukalová and Saša Mouchová of the National Library, except for the last three mentioned. About a thousand copies of each issue were printed and supplied free of charge to those interested. Today they are sought-after collector's items. At the time they were evidence of the serious intentions of the Czech Club. And also evidence of the relatively large number of translations being published in Czechoslovakia despite the rigid opposition of the regime, although each new book was a hard-won victory over the official cultural policy.

If we could use a dual projection technique, we could show how the Czech PEN Club led a double existence, beginning in 1964 when the German writers section was set up within the Exiled Writers PEN Club. The section seems to have had the most members and also to have been the most active of all the groups in exile. In the first elections, Czech and Slovak writers were given important posts in the leadership of the section. Under the chairmanship of the Hungarian K. G. Werner, Antonín Kratochvil, literary critic and historian as well as essayist, was elected vice-chairman. He then followed the Slovak Gaston Hally and the Prague German writer K. M. Ruda as general secretary of the section. He in turn was followed in that post by Rudolf Ströbinger, who chaired the section from the eighties. Among the members of the committee were Jaroslav Dresler, Julius Firt, G. Gruberová-Goepfertová, Imrich Kruzliak, Jaroslav Strnad, Karel Drobeček, Josef Holman and K. M. Ruda, and from 1967 Antonín Měšťan. K. G. Werner was followed as chairman by Gabriel Laub.

Quoting 1964 as the year when the German section of the exile PEN Club was set up does not mean to suggest that good work was not done by our exiled authors in the preceding years. In 1956, for example, the year of the Czechoslovak Writers Congress in Prague, Antonín Kratochvil published an anthology of prose by exiled writers, entitled *The Exile's Penny*, financed by the Association of Czechoslovak Political Refugees in Germany. Even earlier Peter Demetz had published a selection of poems by exiles, *The Invisible Home,* in the Editions Sokolova, Paris. It included verse by Ivan Blatný, Karel Brušák, Jaroslav Dresler, Pavel Javor, Ivan Jelínek, Junius, Jiří Karnet, Jiří Klan, František Kovárna, Jiří Lederer, František Listopad, Antonín Měšťan, Milada Součková, Miroslav Tůma and Jaroslav Tumlíř. In 1955 another anthology of verse, edited by Antonín Vlach, was published in Vienna by Bohemica Vienensia.

Exile and Exiles... the briefest essay would run to dozens of pages. Continents have been founded by exiles, beginning with the Pilgrims pioneering in America. Yet there is a problem here. The man who leaves one existence behind him and starts a new life in another country, never to return: is he an exile? And are there not regions full of returned exiles, even if they were called emigrants?

Those who were forced into exile are a different case. Yet again: among them are some whose lives were in danger, while others who would have stayed on, if they could have stayed the course, but who could not and would not support the pressures that staying on involved. Yet again: there are individual exiles whose steps turn outwards and who are not typical, and there are those who are thrown up by a wave of exile in company with others, linked together by fate or religion and sharing their exile. A seed-box of questions, the equation exile-exiles.

"The image of the poet accursed, the outcast artist, the creator set apart by the act of creation itself, is undoubtedly pure romanticism. But the reality of that unreal thing, creation, is surely exile. It is not chance that makes almost all the 'fathers' of modern thought exiles either by choice or by fate. The modern novel is dominated by Proust, a voluntary outcast, and Joyce, the Irishman of Trieste and Paris. Modern painting is dominated by Picasso, the Catalonian of Paris, and Klee, a German dying in Switzerland. The modern mind is dominated by Einstein, who ended his life in America, and Freud, who died in London. And from Stravinsky to Boulez exile seems to be the rule in music. The seventh muse? Nine-tenths of this art is the work of permanent exiles or of Americans – those Europeans in exile."

These are the words of the French poet and essayist Claude Roy, who befriended the Czech exiles of 1968–9 and became the friend of Milan Kundera, a Czech writer who today dominates the novel from Paris. Would Kundera have settled there, without the Soviet invasion? The fact that so many outstanding intellectuals came to maturity in exile is pregnant with questions. Is it pure chance that the excellent "Lettres Internationales," more than international since they appear not only in French, but in Italian and Spanish, German and Russian, Serbo-Croat and finally Czech as well, has A. J. Liehm for godfather, a Czech exile since 1969? If Czech (or Slovak) intellectuals are exiled, between the fateful dates 1948 and 1968, they are exiles by choice as well as by fate. This is an eloquent testimony to the spiritual poverty of the regime that drove them out. And what of their brethren, the "inner exiles" who stayed at home and suffered, often along with their families, and were silenced, jailed and even executed? The wave of exiles from 1948 to 1968 represents a powerful and fertile explosion. There emerged nine publishing houses in exile, with an admirable list of titles. Škvoreckýs' Sixty-Eight Publishers in Toronto account for 225; Müller's Index for 174 titles in Cologne; the Munich Homeless Poetry of Strož published 108 titles, not counting extra editions; Confrontace of Zurich has a hundred publications to its credit, London

Rozmluvy 100, Opus Bonum in Frankfurt 31, Arkýř in Munich 16 with 35 titles issued by CCC Books Munich. The Rome Christian Academy (Studium and Vigilie) can boast a hundred and six.

The very number of editions that publishers managed to place on the market in foreign countries is amazing, but it is no less remarkable that all these publications were literary in character, whether written in exile or "at home." This gives the picture. Not only the picture of individuals like the Škvoreckýs, Müller, Strož and the rest, but that of a culture that defended itself after "biafrization" by creating new works, sending the smoke from burned books into nothingness with the breath of the spirit. All who took part, whether as writers, editors, copyists or smugglers of these texts, were creating something new in history. One of them, Antonín Kratochvil, published his *Dichter ohne Heimat* (Poets without Homeland) in 1970; he was one of those who helped to form a homeland. The Hungarian writer Kasimir G. Werner, chairman of the PEN Club in exile, said in his introduction to the book: "The poet's work is his spiritual homeland, the poetry of the exile is the spirit of his homeland." It is as if we heard the echo of the old illusion that "it is the role of the PEN Club to preserve the continuity of the creature, man, despite autarchy and totalitarianism in our age." K. G. Werner wrote: "We believe that the free spirit will conquer frontiers and walls, for if we did not have this faith, we would long ago have been lost. "Like no other writers, we in exile know that we are not here for ourselves alone, but to bear witness."

There is something hidden beneath that witness, something that has always been exacted, from Ovid and Seneca to Blatný: "The sadness of exile, the autumnal memories, the Indian summers of hope, the illusions, the dreams and the homesickness. That is something that no living soul can construe as a picture of moral depravity." The exile Egon Hostovský broadcasting in November 1954.

And as if adding to those words, the one-time chairman of International PEN, Charles Morgan, wrote: "There is no place among us for those writers who have become the instruments of tyranny. Those writers persecuted by tyranny have the right to our help and protection. It is a fundamental duty of the PEN Club to attain a state of affairs where there are no poets in exile."

There are coincidences and chance happenings in life that can be truly fatal. In the tragic summer of 1968 Jiřina Tůmová died; she had cared for the Czech Club for forty-three years, ever since its foundation. It is thanks to her above all that there is any history of our PEN Club to write. Nothing could have been achieved without her untiring activity, no event organized, no guests from abroad, no lectures or publications; often it was she who had the ideas. The Czech Club always had a chairman, secretary, treasurer and committee members, all of them elected, not nominated, but they were subject to change. Day-to-day Club life contained an element of uncertainty; Jiřina Tůmová, executive secretary, was our fixed point. Nor was that only in Prague and for Prague. The executive center of International PEN in London, and Clubs in other lands, all knew her voice on the phone and the letters she wrote. Besides all that happens and is inevitably carried away on the tide, she left us something of permanent value: the PEN Archives. The boxes of papers preserved by the Museum of Literature on Strahov in Prague and at Staré Hrady town are the record of tireless and reliable daily efforts over the years. Together with A. M. Tilschová and K. J. Beneš she protected the archives (and the property of the PEN Club) from the Gestapo, and it was undoubtedly thanks to her that the Club survived the fifties. In those difficult days her modest and retiring character worked wonders, vigilant and with an eye for the one person in the totalitarian bureaucratic web who would be capable of rational or even imaginative thinking, and to whom she or someone else could turn for help for PEN. She was well-fitted for the job not only by her knowledge of languages (she spoke French, English, German, Polish and Serbo-Croatian) but by her tact, clear-sightedness and devotion. She gave her all to the Club. From the day the Nazis executed her husband Vladimír Tůma for his underground activity (she, too, was imprisoned for the same reason), there was no other partner in her life. She devoted herself to her literary interests and her translations, of which the most important was probably

The Silent Sea by Vercors. He served as her criterion of commitment without party bias, its core principled anti-fascism. She had worked in the theater as a young woman, but there was nothing in her of the "variety girl"; she had a sense of order, of a sort of creative stagecraft. She was considerate to everyone, almost sweet, with her "dears" and "darlings." Her death and burial passed almost unnoticed in the hectic days when the "fraternal armies" charged into the Hyde Park debating club that Prague had become.

1968: only someone who keeps a careful diary can say now who came and who refused to come and who died that summer. Most of the intellectuals round the world were on the side of the Prague Spring, even such Sovietophiles as Aragon and Pablo Neruda. In 1938 various self-proclaimed democrats were on the side of Munich and hurried away from the Czechoslovakia they had professed to admire, like Jules Romains, the star of the Prague PEN Congress. (In 1941, when the international executive committee was preparing for the 17th Congress, as Victor Fischl reported, they were faced with "the delicate task of electing a new international chairman and deposing the current one, Jules Romains.") There was no such volte-face after the Soviet-led invasion. The hard-line conservatives on the left, the hawks, continued to serve their masters with their usual good manners. When Elisaveta Bagryana, the Bulgarian poet well-known in the Prague PEN Club, celebrated her seventy-fifth birthday in her native Sliven, several Bulgarian intellectuals told the Czech delegate: "Don't think we're going to let you break away from the socialist camp." After Fidel Castro's fanatical outburst to the Cuban National Artists, Nicolás Guillén no longer wrote to Prague or answered our letters. But Juan Goytisolo, Carlos Fuentes, and even García Marquéz came to Prague to express their solidarity with us in person after August 1968. "Words like progressive and reactionary, left- and right-wing, have lost their meaning in what has happened to Czechoslovakia," they said in discussion. Graham Greene could not miss Prague. He was no longer young, but when Smrkovský told him his timetable was so full that he could only see him at half past seven in the morning, Greene cheerfully accepted, even though he had been up half the night before, talking to Hoffmeister and other writers. Smrkovský's secretary was worried by the visit, which could only put Srmkovský into even greater disfavor with the Russians. Everything he did was to tell against him. Claude Roy, who also came to Prague then, later wrote: "It took a lot of hard work before the Czechs acquired the hatred of the Russians they feel today, and 'socialism' unveiled the ugly face we now know." The intellectuals of West Germany played a strange role after the invasion by our "fraternal allies." The support they gave to Czechoslovak culture threw an ironic light on Soviet propaganda with its stories of tens of thousands of German agents slipping into Czechoslovakia disguised as tourists. Heinrich Böll, chairman of International PEN, would have found it hard to disguise himself – he was too well-known in the world.

In the dark days of the second occupation of Czechoslovakia the Prague Club ceased to exist. Jiřina Tůmová's function had passed to Marta Kadlečíková, but she was not allowed to throw herself into the job with her characteristic vehemence. She was a recent recipient of an international short story prize. The clubs abroad had her address, and she received the documents and information they sent, but she could only put them tidily away instead of feeding the life of the Club with them. This was the time of "normalization," as this latest suppression of freedom was called. Normalization set about breaking up everything that existed in the country, everything that had been slowly built up during the years of the "thaw," to supply the natural needs of cultural life, built up with all the skill and cunning, courage and self-sacrifice that those involved could muster. They had not only resisted totalitarianism all those years, but had won back things of real value.

In the years before the war, the Czechoslovak Left was not totalitarian in its attitude, and even among Communist intellectuals various conceptions existed side by side and were democratically defended by those committed to them. It was part of the European tradition of democracy, which had given birth to the trade union movement, cooperatives, societies and political parties. The grim fifties, under pressure from dogmatic minds trained in the land of the Soviets, taught a hard lesson not only to non-communist democratic critics, but to many intellectuals active in their professional groups, in publishing and in the universities. Zhdanov's ideas conflicted sharply with their needs and interests, and turned them against that creed. The process this set in motion in 1956 was thus one of revitalization in this sense.

Normalization gradually put an end to all this, using the basest methods and combinations of cunning tricks and compulsion. The principal target was the Writers Union, which in the early sixties, led by such writers as Eduard Goldstücker, Jan Procházka and Jaroslav Seifert, had become a hothouse of critical ideas and the institutional means by which they could be put into practice. *Literární Noviny* (the literary weekly), the paper of the intellectual revival, was attacked daily for years, intrigued against with attempts at an official takeover and finally reconquered. With its circulation of 150,000 it was a powerful seat of opposition to the authorities, and after it published the "Two thousand words" it was a threat to the whole "socialist camp" and especially to Brezhnev's Soviet Union – a threat that had to destroyed. And when the invasion came, the premises of the Writers Union, of the publishing house, of *Literární Noviny,* and other periodicals, as well as the Literary Fund, were all occupied by the military, and held for a long time. Step by step this literary power center was broken down, until only a powerless Writers Union was left to be dissolved. It went out of existence. It took a few years before a handful of quislings headed by Jan Kozák, Ivan Skála, Josef Taufer and other dogmatists patched together another Union made up of submissive souls. It lasted until the autumn of 1989, but after the "velvet" revolution it had no place in our lives.

The PEN Club could but profit from this process of revival, and its leading members had their place in it, but by its very nature, the Club could not take the initiative. For this reason the "normalizers" did not turn their weapons against it. The Club could perhaps have lived on, but only at a price: the public approval of the aid brought by the "fraternal armies" and of the whole normalization process. This of course the PEN Club, hitherto actively progressive, could not accede to, and so it suppressed itself. For years. The chairman of the Czech Club was one of the writers most victimized and treated to the most treacherous reprisals. Not, however, in that function, but as a leading figure in the Association of Cultural Organizations, whose members, the various professional societies, were among the most radical supporters of the cultural revival. There was no way Adolf Hoffmeister could fail to be wiped off the cultural map.

He was involved with the PEN Club from the very start, almost as much as with Devětsil, which he helped to found. He was accepted for membership at the second committee meeting, in 1925, when he was twenty-three. Twelve years later, as one of those intellectuals who took a stand against fascism, he said in a lecture on art addressed to young people: "We have come to you, not to ask you to help us, but to accept us in your midst." This was always Hoffmeister's ambition, and one he clung to all his life. At thirty-two he still found it difficult to say who he was, but in 1962 the Europa Litteraria described him as "poeta, pittore, caricaturista, dramaturge e cineasta." They omitted to say that he was also a university professor, an ambassador, a ministerial head of department, a prisoner in jail, a traveler and a frequent delegate, a member of societies, university vice-chancellor and a firebrand – and least of all what he was trained to be, a lawyer. As a writer he had no trouble fitting into the PEN Club, for his travel writings are all informed with the spirit of interplay of artists and of nations; *The Unwilling Tourist, Telescope, The American Swing, Made in Japan,* and *Skyscrapers in the Jungle.* It was this same spirit that gave birth to his "Likenesses and Prefigurations," his caricatures and character drawings and his cartoon films. Affinity with the avant-garde was a permanent mark of his work – the avant-garde that was almost synonymous with fun in his eyes. Talking about the crisis in caricature, in 1935, he said (perhaps quoting Vančura): "Yes, I feel sad in this gloomy Bohemia, a land without inspiration and without affection, among people who are always racking their brains and worrying. You are cold and stern and no passion can touch you except for one, and that is the most destructive of all, except for the passion of reason." Yet Hoffmeister did so much for this country, in all corners of the earth, for he had friends everywhere. And besides that he made great fun for his country. When Husák's normalization regime ensured that Czech culture lay in ruins, as Hoffmeister complained, he suffered the fate of many other intellectuals: not allowed to publish, to exhibit, to speak in public. And so he set to work, even harder than usual, because he was a hard worker in normal life. He envied no one, but others envied him, especially the lazy ones who forgot why he was working so hard. And so after the liquidation of the *Literární Noviny* and the art journals and the Unions and the art schools he buried himself in his studio in the Myší Díra ["Mouse Hole" – a small street near the spot where the new "Hoffmeister hotel" was built] and made dozens of collages. He was not allowed to exhibit them to the public, and so he hung them on the walls of his home, and since he was not allowed to invite the public to the opening, he invited his friends and those interested, in small groups, day by day. This was the time when Vlasta Chramostová invented the "home theater," for the same reasons; Hoffmeister invented the "home exhibition rooms." He was happy in his misfortune, and drove out to his country cottage with one of his sons and some friends, and there he quietly died. It was his heart. But what was it that killed his heart? Verses by Miroslav Holub were read at his cremation ceremony.

No more was needed to show that the Czech PEN Club had been buried with its chairman, just as thirty years earlier with Karel Čapek. And as then, it did not dissolve itself, it did not give up, but simply went silent. The powers that were did not prohibit it, they would probably have been happy to "allow its activities to continue" – at a shameful price. For that the Prague Club had too honorable a past and too courageous a present, and too many members active in exile. And so once again, as under the previous foreign occupation, the Czech PEN Club became an exile.

There were several centers, of course, in Canada, the United States, England and France; and just as the continuity of the banned Czech Club was ensured during the war by the London center, now it was the German center that spoke for mute Prague. There were two reasons for this: it was in West Germany that the greatest number of exiled writers gathered both after 1948 and after 1968. And it was in West Germany that they found the greatest moral and material support.

This was a section of the PEN Club in exile that had its headquarters in London, and embraced writers settled in all the German-speaking lands, not only West Germany, and all exiles, not only the Czechs. There were the Hungarians exiled after 1956, either immediately after the uprising or in the years that followed. Gyula Hay settled in Switzerland when he was freed from his Hungarian prison, and it was there that he wrote his remarkable memoirs, *Born 1900*. Naturally the Hungarian writers were the moving spirit of the section, above all the first chairman, K. G. Werner.

The "PEN Center for Writers in Exile," which embraced writers from Central and Eastern Europe, was recognized as a full member of International PEN, with the right to send two delegates to meetings of the international executive committee, to International PEN Congresses, and so on. In the course of time they acquired an international secretary, and for a long time, roughly 1960–1980, this was Pavel Tigrid, who had settled in France.

The German-speaking section was very active in publishing and editing, on individual initiative, but it was encouraging and inspiring for the whole of the exile Club.

For Czech writers "at home," deprived of any possibility of publishing their work unless they were the darlings of the regime, members of the official Writers Union and supporters of the government, the publishing houses in exile played an important material role. We have already recalled their numerous editions, which together with samizdat "publication" at home helped to preserve the intellectual capacity of creative minds in exile and at home. Having named the editors of Czech literature in exile, we should now name those of the samizdat "presses": Ludvík Vaculík, Jan Vladislav (until he too emigrated), and Vladimír Pistorius, to mention only the most active, and with them their invaluable aides, reliable and courageous, copying texts and smuggling them abroad: Jiřina Šiklová, Marie Jirásková, Wolfgang Scheuer, J. Jelínek.

An important role in the preservation of samizdat and exile publications, both Czech and Slovak, in the difficult times of dictatorship, was played by the Scheinfeld-Schwarzenberg Czechoslovak Documentation Center for Independent Literature. That it is possible to study this literature today is mainly due to the work of the historian Vilém Prečan who established and directed the Center.

International PEN gave continued systematic aid and encouragement to Czech and Slovak literature in its banishment; for example, the executive committee meeting in London on December 12–13th, during the darkest days, when the chairman Heinrich Böll described the situation in Czechoslovakia after four years of "normalization" as a "cultural graveyard." In the discussion that followed, ways and means of helping Czechoslovak writers were put forward. The delegates from the socialist countries present at the meeting could not deny this apt description of the state of affairs. Delegates from the PEN Center for Writers in Exile played a significant role at this meeting: Julian Gorkin, George Mikes, Ivan Jelínek and Pavel Tigrid all spoke in the discussion. The Czech Club was regarded as "sleeping," not as dissolved. The West German PEN Club proposed sending an official delegation from International PEN to investigate the possibility of reopening the Czech Club. The attitude of the executive committee towards the Chilean PEN Club was significant: it was given six weeks to make its intentions known. It was agreed that Arthur Miller would pay a private visit to Prague to talk to blacklisted writers there and report back to the general secretary.

In the epilogue to his anthology *Dichter ohne Heimat,* Antonín Kratochvil, one of its leading protagonists, dates the birth of Czech and Slovak exile literature in the fifties. He wrote then (1970) that in the twenty years of the existence of this literature, over six hundred titles had been published, representing the only free literary production of the years of the personality cult and socialist realism (1948–1957). We would agree with his periodization, but the number of those publications is surprising. However, it is necessary to define the term "free literary production," and particularly whether it can only exist where the writer enjoys civic freedom. Under similar conditions, for instance towards the end of the first world war in 1918, or during the Nazi occupation, there was writing which was undoubtedly free, inspired with a spirit of rebellion against oppression and the longing for freedom, although it was not free to be published. Even so, these writers bore a heavy risk and had to have the courage of their convictions. This was also true for the writers of cryptoliterature, typical of such times, whose readers were on the same wavelength. An example from the years of "normalization" was the volume of verse, *On the Slivers of Freedom*. For if freedom is something that has to be fought for, it cannot automatically follow from the status of the writer: it is possible to think of work written in conditions of absolute freedom, and well-written, but where the spiritual tension created by the necessity of struggling for intellectual freedom is entirely lacking. The half-century of abnormal conditions hypocritically designated as "normalization" must be clearly and inexorably analyzed; it will be the duty of such an analysis to distinguish clearly between genuinely creative writing and what merely passes for creative, the calculated imitation, the loud-voiced proclamation of freedom slogans. The task is all the more urgent in that today we have three separate literatures to be submitted to a single scale of values.

The German section of the exile PEN Club certainly did its best in this direction, in the difficult conditions of exile and without the necessary source materials. In April 1982 a significant conference was held in Bonn, at which the Czech critic Dr. Kratochvil spoke on "What Truth and Humanity Mean For Literature." The Polish theater producer J. Hoffmann and Olga Ribowska from Riga discussed the theater and drama criticism, while Dr. Gerber talked about the crisis in the West German theater.

A year later the exile PEN Club held its international congress at Eichholz near Bonn, on the theme of "Political Exile and Contemporary Literature As Reflected In Exile Writing." Then in May 1985 a discussion was held at Gaisbach (Oberkirch) entitled "Europaische Kulturpolitik – Motor der europaischen Integration." The political questions which troubled the nineties were already coming to the fore. But what have they to do with culture, and what is the place of culture in that context? In the words of the Italian sociologist Umberto Campagnolo: "Culture cannot be determined by an individual act of will. On the other hand the individual can influence culture indirectly by furthering social harmony. From this point of view moral and political action is decisive for cultural life. The value of the nation and the place it takes in history thus depend on the degree of social integration, which is itself the more fertile the more numerous the elements evoked and maintained in harmonious unity by moral law. Thus the age and variety of traditions are the main factor of social integration, thereby justifying their identification with culture. For many people culture means awareness of the ideas of the past. Nevertheless the only true culture is that which foretells and prepares new social values."

Despite all the efforts made in the West, international politics still acted as a retarding factor in this sphere. Helsinki assured the Soviet Union its existing frontiers, while the Soviet acknowledgment of human rights was no more than a formal gesture. It took another ten years before the degeneration of neo-Stalinism produced Gorbachev and his policy of genuine, not mere sham, rapprochement. For cultural life in Eastern Europe those ten years meant continued bondage, and the birth of dissent and samizdat "publishing." Meanwhile signs of a new quality were appearing among writers in exile: the work of Miłosz, Kundera, or Brodsky transcended the traditions of their native lands. A trend towards integration could be seen in western culture, promoted by exiled spirits. National traditions were no longer the mainspring of new values.

At the same time, however, the increased use of mechanical means of reproduction and distribution brought about a qualitative change in cultural life and resulted in a wave of unoriginal work, slavish imitation and primitive imposture, bringing with it a lack of respect for traditional forms of culture such as reading, amateur activities and so on. Gradually what Finkielkraut calls "the defeat of thought" established itself.

Life goes on, and when the political break came, the fall of totalitarianism, of the whole "socialist bloc" and its Third World offshoots, conditions were very different in cultural life from those which accompanied the rise of fascism, Nazism, Stalinist communism, Franco's falangism and all the varieties of totalitarianism over half a century ago. Today we seem to see a revival in the different forms of fundamentalism, particularly in religion.

At the end of the eighties in "normalized" Czechoslovakia, cracks began to appear in the monolithic authority governing cultural life; the hermetic seals crumbled to show party bigwigs who seemed want to look respectable in modern salons. As if they were letting in by the back door all that they had systematically suffocated since 1948 and even more determinedly from 1968 – the free creative spirit, "that bloweth where it listeth." A breath of air was to be allowed to stir the fetid stuffings of a country where no one was ever heard to mention "overtaking the West" anymore, so general and obvious was the hopeless decrepitude.

It was no accident that "they" invoked the tradition of the PEN Club, the traditional nonpolitical cultural organization for the world of politics. PEN was to be resurrected, and the impetus came from two very dissimilar quarters. On the one hand, the Minister of Culture, perhaps suspecting he was to be the last, but hardly expecting to be forgotten so soon, invited four members of the old PEN Club Committee (almost the last survivors) to meet him in the summer of 1989. In accordance with the ritual of many decades' standing, representatives of the Writers Union were present, in this case Mrs. Adlová and the chairman of the Union, the poet Miroslav Válek, who was also a former Minister of Culture. He it was, in 1969, who replied to complaints about the disastrous state of our cultural life with the brief words: "You should have stood behind Husák." He was still able to publish a compendious anthology of his verse, thanks to the Cuban Cultural Center.

The Minister had carefully worked out his strategy. There were two of the old PEN Club cadres for whom Václav Havel was a thorn in the flesh, and who were at great pains to condemn

him as an imperialist agent: Dr. František Kafka and Ema Řezá-
čová. The remaining two PEN Club members, Lumír Čivrný and
Josef Nesvadba, naturally refused to take this stand, and so the
carefully planned meeting went awry. The excuse the Minister
found to explain his action was that it was too late for the plenary session of the PEN Club to meet – according to the rules it
met in the first quarter of the year. It did not bother him in the
least that this had not happened for the last twenty years.

The other official impetus for the resurrection of the PEN
Club came from the Writers Union. These people, accustomed
for the last twenty years to the normality of abnormality, suddenly felt the need for the PEN Club, and even wrote to London,
to the international center, to say so. There, of course, they knew
perfectly well what was going on, and what had happened in the
past, and quietly shelved the matter.

It was not until the third attempt that there was any chance
of success. This was made by a group of blacklisted writers who
felt that in the deepening bog threatening to engulf Czech writers and Czech literature, an organization was imperative, and
that in body and in spirit this should be the PEN Club. They
chose a democratic approach, which nevertheless was a risk in
those days: they issued a call for the revival of the PEN Club.
The chairman of the revived Club, Ivan Klíma, recalls that they
decided on this approach because it could be acceptable to the
powers that be, and on the other hand they could hardly, in the
circumstances, reject it. Ten dissident writers (but not the most
provocative) were chosen to sign the letter, along with ten from
the "grey zone" (writers who were allowed to publish but not to
be members of the Writers Union), and ten from the Union itself.
Surviving members of the old dormant PEN Club also signed:
Čivrný and Nesvadba, mentioned above; Marta Kadlečíková,
who was officially recognized by International PEN; Hela Volanská, who was ill at the time, and Jiří Mucha, who was to become
chairman of the temporary committee. Before that could be
elected, of course, meetings had to be held and decisions taken,
but the former were still illegal, and the authorities did their
best to prevent them from taking place – on August 1, 1989, for
instance, Václav Havel was arrested on his way to a meeting in

the Chodov Tower, Milan Jungmann at another point, and Jan Trefulka at a third, as we are told by one of the organizers of the meeting, the poet and current committee member, Jana Štroblová. That autumn there was a meeting at Jiří Mucha's home, attended by Václav Havel, Ivan Klíma, Hana Bělohradská, Marta Kadlečíková, Jana Štroblová, Daniela Fischerová, Josef Nesvadba, Karel Šiktanc and Lumír Čivrný, and yet even in its death throes the totalitarian regime fought back. The Sunday after the brutal attack on students, Friday, the 17th of November, the newly elected committee had arranged to meet in Karel Šiktanc's flat, but the security police occupied the ground floor of the house, arrested people as they arrived and took them off to the local police station for questioning, including Jana Červenková, Lumír Čivrný, Daniela Fischerová, Milan Jungmann and others. What the police most wanted to know was whether and how the PEN Club was reporting the student massacre abroad.

The proper revival of the PEN Club – in accordance with its statutes – took place at a plenary session on January 4, 1990, in the ancient house At the Sign of the Melon, in the Old Town. A new committee was formally elected, with Jiří Mucha as chairman.

At the end of May, 1990, a busload of Czech (and of course Moravian) writers left National Street for the Dobříš chateau. As they passed into the main courtyard an unusual sight met their eyes. From the other side of the courtyard there advanced another group, greeting the visitors from Prague. These were German writers who had invited their Czech colleagues to take part in their regular group readings, and exchange views. It was the German "Group 47," who had waited twenty years for this moment; arranged long ago, the meeting was considered undesirable, abnormal under the "normal" Husák regime. Two exiled Czech writers presided, Tomáš Kosta and Jiří Gruša, who was so young that he could have no memory of relations between Czech and German writers between the two world wars, when the Mann brothers, Gerard Hauptmann and others were the guests of the Czech PEN Club, headed then by Karel Čapek and A. M.

Tilschová. The guests of this day were headed by Jiří Mucha, and their welcome came from the "neutral" Jiří Gruša, while the focus of the meeting was of course the German writers, headed by the founder of Group 47, Hans Werner Richter. Gruša described the group as being on the way out, but at its founding in 1947, it was committed both in the historical and in the literary sense. The presence of Günther Grass confirmed this; he declared his model to be Alfred Doblin, an independent left-wing personality, while what he feared was the descent of humanity into poverty and the destruction of the environment, and what he felt as a menace was Eurocentrism. He ended on an unemotional note: "I am glad that although the weaker, we writers have shown the greater resilience." It turned out that the Germans read their work, as was their custom at these meetings, and so did the Czechs, contrary to their custom. There were times when even the Germans understood Czech, at least in the clownish form Ludvík Vaculík gave it.

This meeting enriched the contacts formed during the late sixties, when writers on both sides of the frontier helped each other to resist their tyrants. This community in variety, as yet little analyzed by literary historians, has not yet died away. Today there is not only the Czech PEN Club behind them, but also the Goethe Institute, with its remarkable efforts to reconstruct the triple culture of pre-war Prague, long destroyed.

As if the year 1990 was destined to revive old relationships, the Croatian PEN Club center in Zagreb decided to hold a congress of the PEN Clubs of the "Pentagon" countries, on November 1st, in Dubrovnik. The theme "What Is The Place of Literature In the New Europe?" gave writers from two traditional European centers and from three newly established as European the chance to declare their unity in variety and to give evidence of it. The outcome was a common condemnation of nationalism: there was no voice raised in its defense, yet the writers were not able to forestall the destruction that was in the offing. Ancient Dubrovnik, where as long ago as the sixteenth century the Renaissance scholar Marina Držiće condemned barbarity, became its victim. Even the solidarity of the "Pentagon" intellectuals made itself heard only mildly, when the Yugoslav army (i.e. of Serbia and Montenegro) began shooting up the treasures of Dubrovnik's Renaissance architecture. When they organized this PEN meeting, the Croats were commendably trying to revive memories of the Dubrovnik Congress in 1933, which sharply condemned the Nazis for burning books, and the choice of venue for 1993 stressed this. But it was not to be, for nationalist militarism found its way to the Adriatic and surrounding regions, and with its policy of ethnic cleansing seemed set to rival the Holocaust. In 1990 the Czech PEN Club welcomed the chance to send two delegates, Čivrný and Karpatský. By the spring of 1993 this would be more than impossible.

The November PEN Club congress held in Vienna in 1991 was extremely well structured and carried through; it was a demanding symposium with four literary sessions, each with its specific program: The World of Literature and the Real World; The Other in the New Structures of Freedom; Ego; and Mondialism. Inspiring speakers from every continent had their say, but those from Eastern and Central Europe were in the majority. Hanuš Karlach, secretary of the Prague center, spoke on "From the certainties of non-freedom to the uncertainties of freedom"; he was one of those for whom the courage to ask questions, to probe and to think stand higher than claims to know all the answers.

What ordinary citizens note goes for the history of the PEN Club, too. Whereas for twenty totalitarian years, since 1968, time seemed to stand still, the stagnant water of the years never stirring, after the "revolution" time changed and began racing along, the years pass all too soon, and here we are in the fourth year of freedom. The first swallows were the Book Fairs with Michael March, the American poet: in the autumn, instead of swallows, scholars gathered from all over the world to discuss Czech language and literature. Round-table discussions on literature were no longer a rare occurrence – yet what was still rare was the appearance of good books, even older ones, not to speak of new ones.

In the footsteps of Czech writer Alois Jirásek and his book *From Bohemia to the End of the World*, a delegation went from the Czech PEN Club to the international congress in Santiago de Compostella in Spanish Galicia, that is to say in the same direction as Europe set out half a millennium ago in search of adventure.

It was a victorious and yet painful undertaking. It meant the discovery and at the same time the almost complete disappearance of one human race, and the almost complete destruction of a great human civilization. Europe, so self-assured, discovered a continent which she changed to her own image so completely that it disappeared and became a new world in the sense that it negated the old world it had been. All that was left were fragments of architecture (some so deep in the jungle that they have not yet been discovered, whether for better or worse), ironical comments bringing to man's notice how strange and unrepeatable that world had been, the original old new world.

Today, Europe – both the European and that spread over all the continents – is awakening to a realization. As if in a sort of archeological ecstasy, she uncovers strata after strata of time, looking back into the unseeable, yet as a part of contemporary experience. Europe is becoming aware of the crisis in its own culture, but in one respect this crisis differs from all previous ones in the threat that it may become the final crisis, the last lethal phase of man's earth.

Even if this does not happen, Europe will face a critical situation because other, non-European cultures have arrived on the scene and will not be driven out. Thus our culture, confronted with the others in the world, is bound to see as it were the mirror image of our past. If Europe is to achieve a state from which the future can emerge, she must go through with this experience to the bitter end. The burden of survival and the pain of seeking is her fate.

The PEN Club was founded 70 years ago to work for the brotherhood of peoples by bringing writers together. Today the peoples need to be protected from themselves; culture must be strong enough to save humanity. If only the executive committee of International PEN could get from a heavenly computer center a microprocessor for all its clubs, and this microprocessor would apply the writers' activities to the whole of each nation...

It would not be reasonable to expect the history of the Czech PEN Club to show a single line of development or even to be monotonous. It has moved onwards in a series of radical breaks, and we can best try to divide these 70 years into shorter and quite distinctive stages.

The first ten years from 1925 are probably closest to the idea of the PEN Club which its English pioneers professed and which was accepted by the founders of the Czech Club. Then the defense of national culture became more urgent, culminating in the 1938 congress. A unifying characteristic of the PEN Club throughout its existence under the First Republic was its monopoly of cultural contacts with other countries.

During the years after Munich and the death of Karel Čapek, after the expected prohibition of Club activity by the Gestapo in 1942, until the plenary session in November 1945, the Czech center was in exile in London, chaired by František Langer.

After a short attempt to continue in its pre-war traditions, the Czech PEN Club entered into a dormant phase after February 1948. Its aim was survival, but its efforts to remain an island of cultural individuality despite the totalitarian pressures deserve our respect.

1956 shook the monolith of Stalinism to its foundations, everywhere in the world, and the courageous stand taken by Czech writers opened up new vistas for the Czech PEN Club in the period of the "thaw" and the Prague Spring. We could appear once more on the world stage.

A new blow from without, and the PEN Club was muffled once more, this time of its own accord, when Husák's "normalization" followed on the heels of the invasion of Czechoslovakia by Soviet troops. Once again the torch was handed on to Czech writers in exile, this time based primarily in West Germany. An important aspect of their literary output was its tendency to look forward to the future.

The interest shown in reviving the Czech PEN Club, in the summer of 1989, was a harbinger of the events of November which led to the collapse of the totalitarian regime and the "velvet" revolution. The general meeting of the PEN Club on January 4, 1990, held in an atmosphere of freedom, marked the beginning of a new phase in its history. It must be left to the future to pass judgment on it.

History has laid a great responsibility on the shoulders of the Czech Club: in November 1994, on the eve of the seventieth anniversary of its founding (February 15, 1925) it will play host to the 61st International PEN Congress. The designated theme is "Literature and Tolerance." In the spring of 1993 preparations for the Congress were set in motion by the Committee, consisting of Jiří Stránský (chairman), Ivan Klíma (vice-chairman), Hana Žantovská (vice-chairwoman), Miroslav Hůle (treasurer), Libuše Ludvíková (Executive Secretary), Antonín Bajaja, Hana Bělohradská, Alexandra Berková, Miroslav Červenka, Jana Červenková, Lumír Čivrný, Václav Daněk, Daniela Fischerová, Josef Hrubý, Hanuš Karlach, František Nepil, Jaroslav Putík, Jana Štroblová and Jaroslav Veis.

LUMÍR
ČIVRNÝ

SOURCES

Archiv PEN Klubu Praha – Památník nár. písemnictví,
Strahov a Staré Hrady.
At the Crossroads of Europe – Prague PEN Club, 1938.
Otakar Vočadlo: *Anglické listy Karla Čapka* – Academia,
Praha 1975.
František Langer: *Byli a bylo* – Čs. spisovatel, Praha 1963.
Otokar Fischer: *Slovo o kritice* – V. Petr, Praha 1947.
Vilém Mathesius: *Možnosti, které čekají* – J. Laichter, Praha
1944.
Karel Čapek: *Anglické listy* – Čs. spisovatel, Praha.
A. Lauermannová-Mikschová: *Lidé minulých dob* – ELK,
Praha.
Translation and translators / A Round-table Discussion, Rome
November 1961 – International PEN, London.
Translation and the theatre / A Round-table discussion of PEN
– Rheims 1963 – Arena, International Writer's Fund of
PEN.
Tradition et modernité / PEN table ronde Budapest 1964/ PEN
Hongrie Corvina, Budapest.
*Literatura brasileira e portuguesa, literatura espanola e latino
americana na Tchecoslováquia desde 1945 até maio de 1960*
– PEN Club tchecoslovaco, Praga 1960.
Literatures of the Near East in Czechoslovakia 1945 – March
1963, Czechoslovak PEN, Prague 1963.
*Scandinavian Literatures in Czechoslovakia from 1945 to May
1964*, Czechoslovak PEN, Prague 1964.
Littératures yougoslaves en tchècoslovaquie 1945–1964 – PEN
Club Tchèque.
La letteratura italiana in Cecoslovacchia dal 1945 al 1964,
PEN Club cecoslovacco, 1965.
American Literature in Czechoslovakia 1945–1965,
Czechoslovak PEN Club, Prague.
La littérature française en Tchécoslovaquie de 1945 à janvier
1964, PEN Club tchècoslovaque, Prague 1964.

Dr. Antonín Kratochvil: *Dichter ohne Heimat – Tschechische und slovakische Exilschriftsteller* – Internationaler PEN Club Zentrum der Exilschriftsteller, München 1970.

Dr. Antonín Kratochvil: *Za ostnanými dráty a minovými poli – vzpomínky a svědectví* I. díl – Mnichov, Brno 1993.

Neue Strukturen der Freiheit – *Literatur als Diagnose und Therapie.* 56. Weltkongres des Internat. PEN 3. 8. Nov. 1991 in Wien – Österreichischer PEN Club, Wien.

Most / The Bridge – Zvláštní vydání – 1. 11. 1990 – Croatian Writers Association, Zagreb.

Jan Čulík: *Seznam publikací vydaných v hlavních exilových nakladatelstvích 1971–1990* – Ústav pro soudobé dějiny, ČSAV, Praha 1992.

Umberto Campagnolo: *Petit dictionnaire pour une politique de la culture* – La Baconnière Neuchâtel Suisse, 1969.

Claude Roy: *Nous* – Gallimard, Paris 1972.

Jiří Gruša: *Cenzura a literární život mimo masmédia* – Ústav pro soudobé dějiny, ČSAV, Praha.

LIST OF THOSE PRESENT
AT THE INAUGURAL GENERAL MEETING,
FEBRUARY 15, 1925

Dr. Hanuš Jelínek
J. Šusta
Vinc. Červinka
Dr. Dohalský
Otokar Fischer
K. Čapek
K. M. Čapek-Chod
A. Lauermannová-Mikschová
Jiří Foustka
Růž. Jesenská
V. Přimda Vladyka
Božena Benešová
Jos. Hrdinová
Rudolf Fuchs
P. Bujnák
Dr. O. Pertold
Goll
Otto Pick
Dr. F. Skácelík

Ing. V. Mixa
M. Pujmanová-Hennerová
Dr. Jan Löwenbach
Dr. O. Vetter
Mathesius
Edmond Konrád
Dr. A. Kraus
Dr. Ferd. Smíšek
Karel Scheinpflug
M. Lesná-Krausová
Dr. Frant. Langer
Dr. Miroslav Rutte
K Z Klíma
V. Lesný
Dr. Rudolf Procházka
Josef Čapek
Josef Kopta
Jaroslav Kvapil

Presenční listina

ustavující schůze Pen. Klubu, konané v Praze, dne 15. února 1925
v Praze, v místnostech klubu Solistů N. D.

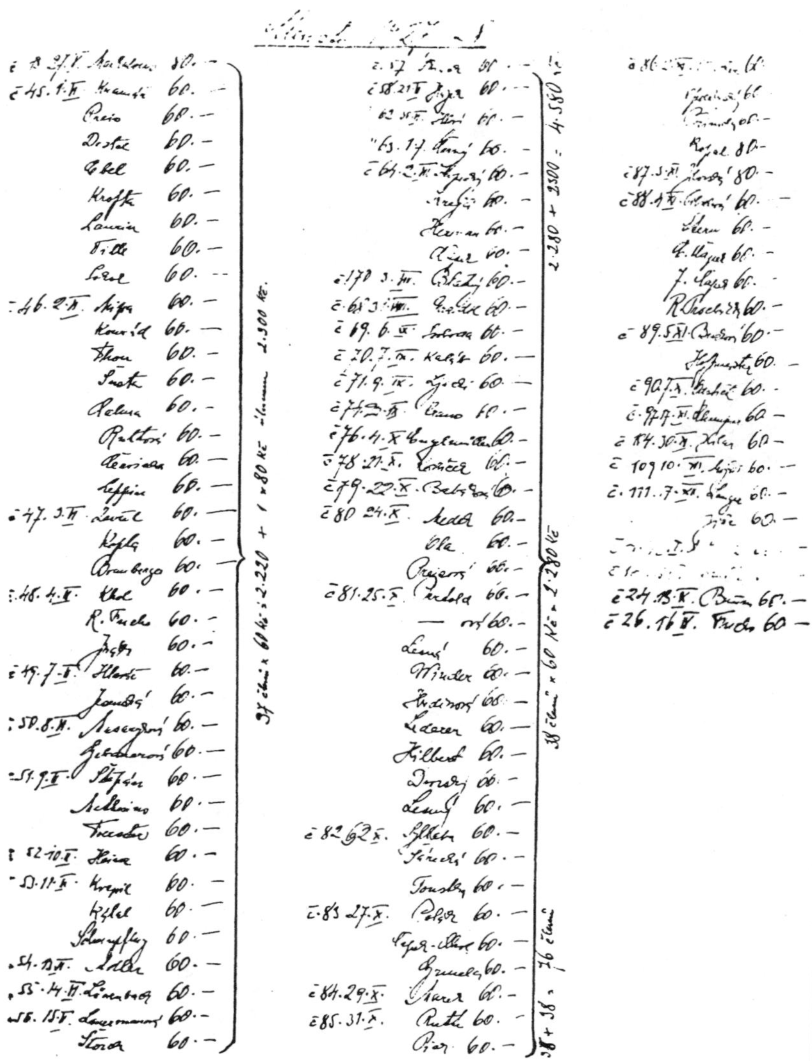

List of members and subscriptions for 1927–8

Karel Čapek, Sholem Asch and František Langer
at a PEN Club evening in Prague

Excellences, Mesdames, Messieurs,

dans la Géographie cordiale de la Tchécoslovaquie il y a, parmi les Scènes de la vie d'après-guerre, un chapitre bien cher à nous tous, intitulé "Georges Duhamel à Prague"; et je vous prie de vous en rappeler quelques pages exquises, par exemple celle sur l'auteur de La lumière, introduit dans notre littérature par Mlle Hrdinová,assistant a la première représentation tchèque de sa belle pièce; ou cette autre: deux écrivains français, hôtes de Mme Lauermannová, deux brillants conférenciers acclamé par un public enthousiasmé; Georges Duhamel, assis à côté de Charles Vildrac, les deux poètes accompagnés par notre ami Jelínek, ou renseignés sur notre théâtre par notre ami Hilar, etc.,etc. - souvenez-vous en somme, je vous en prie, de tout cet art qu'a su exercer l'auteur de La possession du monde, en prenant possession. Il y a plus d'une dizaine d'années, de nos coeurs.

Mesdames, Messieurs, aujourd'hui j'ai le grand honneur de souhaiter la bienvenue, dans le Penclub de Prague, à Monsieur Charles-Roux, ministre de notre jeune république, à Monsieur le ministre Krofta, à Mme Dora Gabé, écrivain bulgare, à M.et Mme.Duhamel, à MM.les professeurs Eisenmann, François, Pruphilet et M.Max Brod, écrivain allemand de Prague qui est venu nous voir pour la première fois - et je voudrais leur dire,'à eux tous,l'assurance de notre joi et de toute notre reconnaissance. Quant à vous, mon illustre confrère, nous saluons en vous non seulement un maître de vos lettres, mais aussi un des frères à nous; ou, pour dire mieux peut-être, nous saluons en vous non seulement un des amis fidèles de notre jeune république, mais surtout un des représentants les plus saisissants, les plus logiques et s'-reins, de la vieille culture de notre vieux pays. Vous nous connaissez assez pour pouvoir juger que dans notre ville intellectuelle beaucoup a changé, mais que les tendances principales et ses qualités dominantes sont restées à peu près les mêmes que dans les premières années de la prétendue paix mondiale. Quant à nous autres, nous avons bien suivi ce que vous appelez vos confessions vagabondes, nous connaissons cette vie de pèlerin que vous avez mené entre Moscou et Chicago, nous savons que vous avez su ne point épargner vos flèches, mais que vous avez continué a aimer les peuples de "l'Europe Mineure". Vous aussi, vous êtes resté le même, seulement, vous êtes devenu plus grand encore, plus profond, plus sévère et plus rempli,de ce sentiment de responsabilité. Spectateur et philosophe, médecin rigoureux d'une humanité malade et gardien consciencieux de la civilisation menacée, vous nous avez prouvé mainte-fois que refléchir, que respirer même, dans ce temps de danger et d'angoisse, veut dire faire de la politique, s'occuper des affaires étrangeres; vous avez démontré qu'il faut, en faisant de la poésie et dans tout le domaine de l'art, préparer l'avenir, qu'il faut bâtir et construire malgré un chaos imminent, qu'il faut croire en l'homme, malgré tous les évangiles et toutes les avantages de la machine.

Mesdames, Messieurs, pour énumérer tous les points où nous d'accord avec notre cher hôte, pour indiquer quelques détails ou quelques nuances dans lesquelles nous différons peut-être, il ne nous faudrait pas seulement prononcer un toast, mais écrire un essai, et l'écrire dans notre langue maternelle: dans celle que Duhamel n'a jamais osé vouloir posséder. Mais il y a une phrase tchèque que nous le prions de vouloir bien retenir: le titre d'un recueil de vers d'un de nos regrettés poètes qui a dit: Ještě jednou se vrátíme. Monsieur et Madame Georges Duhamel, je formule mon voeu au nom des écrivains de Prague: nous désirons que If Mercredi, l'heure de votre départ arrivée, le souvenir du vers cité vous revienne et que vous nous donniez cette promesse: Ještě jednou se vrátíme - nous allons revenir encore une-fois. - Je bois à votre santé, à votre bon voyage, à votre prochaine visite chez nous.

Otokar Fischer
addresses G. Duhamel

H. G. Wells
Sketch by Karel Čapek

Thomas Mann and Salvador de Madariaga
Sketch by Karel Čapek

Paul Valéry and Georges Duhamel
Sketch by Karel Čapek

*Poster for the 16th International PEN Congress
in Prague, 1938*

*Anna Marie Tilschová, chairwoman
of the Prague Club, in 1938*

Karel Čapek
Sketch by Adolf Hoffmeister

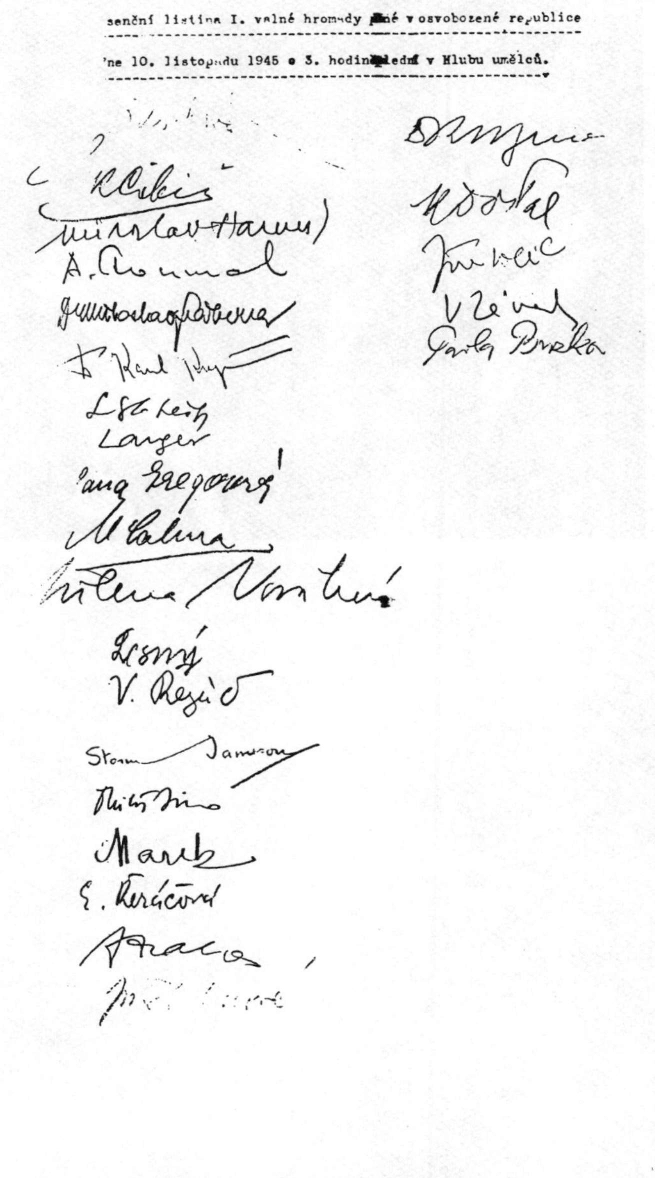
senční listina I. valné hromady v osvobozené republice

'ne 10. listopadu 1945 o 3. hodin odpoledne v Klubu umělců.

List of those present at the general meeting re-establishing the Czech PEN Club, November 11, 1945

*Adolf Hoffmeister, Louis Aragon and Lumír Čivrný
in Paris, 1948*

František Langer
Sketch by
František Muzika

Johannes Urzidil
Sketch by František Muzika

Jiřina Tůmová, David and Mrs. Carver
at Karlštejn in the summer of 1965

Jaroslav Seifert
Sketch by Adolf Hoffmeister

František Hrubín
Sketch by Adolf Hoffmeister

Eduard Goldstücker
Sketch by Adolf Hoffmeister

Václav Havel
Sketch by
Adolf Hoffmeister

Jiří Mucha
Sketch by Adolf Hoffmeister

Josef Škvorecký
Sketch by Adolf Hoffmeister

Ivan Klíma
Sketch by Adolf Hoffmeister

John Steinbeck
Sketch by Adolf Hoffmeister

General Assembly of the Czech Center, January 4, 1990, in Prague

Miroslav Červenka
SYMBOLON

```
        Watch, as I tear this p      oem in two parts.
    The right I give to you, the le     ft I keep for myself.
        It's raining at daw          n and your way
            up to the chap       el forges on and on
    and mine trickles along the g    ully to the stream.
        Years later, when in the c     old cracked earth
            in the poison-soaked     soil beyond the river,
                over each he     ad a different banner,
            we meet, foreign     vaguely familiar faces, –
                left side and     right side
            will sink into place,    line after line
                    like coffin     after coffin
                    on a com     mon
                        car     riage.
```

Miroslav Červenka

THE FUGITIVES' NURSES

Your fame: a wound,
in a hurry, secretly (that's prison
for you) disinfected, wrapped
to the snapping point, so the gauze won't slip
when crawling, killing, when marching full speed.

Again another,
in another dialect, in a different shawl
the bandage reapplied.
Faraway, after yielding, beyond the pass.

MIROSLAV ČERVENKA (1932)
Poet and literary theorist
Prague

Rudolf Matys

TO BEAR FROM THE FUNDAMENTAL

(Marginalia on Tolerance)

The word *tolerance* has its Czech equivalent in the words *snášenlivost* and *snésti* – to bear. The Latin *tolerale* means precisely "to bear from the fundamental, from the beginning." The fundamentality, the basis of the meaning of this word becomes ever more distinct and deepens if we penetrate further into its genetic core: its Greek and Latin stem *fero* has its roots right back in an ancient Indian language, where it is linked with the aspirated *-bher*, which means, in the most general sense, "to bear a burden." The Czech *býti březí* – (of an animal) "to be pregnant" – is also evidently derived from this root – to bear, to contain an embryo.

How deep in meaning is this etymology, how desolately fundamental! And how unconditional, if we measure it by today's functionally flattened, basically only behaviorist explanation of the word!

If tolerance means "to bear from the fundamental," it should not then mean anything dependent on chance circumstances or on individual psychological dispositions. It should stem from the elementary formative ability to bear and carry one's fate as "a natural burden." There are indeed quite a few explanations of all kinds of intolerance, whether interpersonal, ethnic, racial or class, as merely the inability to bear one's genuine lot, accept it and fulfill it within the limits of natural determination and given facts – and with that to admit a consciousness of one's own insignificance. This inability begets hatred and intolerance towards oneself, which in turn makes one susceptible to temptations which offer forgetfulness of self and magnification of the importance of all one's frustrations in identification with the abbreviations of collectivist floods. Deliberation and gradual self-reflection and also patience, "delaying anger" and moderation, which are ethical qualities introduced to the vocabulary of tolerance by the Hebrew of the Old Testament, are replaced by the delight of identification with the anonymous force of the gang, the crowd, the masses. This identification apparently liberates one from the "weight of oneself," but in fact only liberates one from responsibility for oneself and for the ultimate, endlessly distant sense of one's own life. As has been stated many times, the roots of the collective narcissism of nations, races and classes grow in this psychological soil. These roots are the "holy bonds" of origin, blood and earth, which unleash those ominous fires of "eternal returns," and which would like to make history a repetitive discontinuum of false eschatology: "the last battles which flared up." The emblems really are incidental ones and interchangeable. In all of them we see the same self-excesses in which a person reaches beneath himself. Even beneath the animal in himself. The mass Narcissus gazes at himself, together with many others, in the single surface of the swollen mass ego. But in fact he is at that moment blind. The reflection only tells him what he looks like. He likes to believe it, he likes himself for the moment, until he is pushed under the surface...

Pascal rightly places man in a precarious position "between an animal and an angel." This duality, this tragic and creative contradiction, this paradoxical ambiguity of humankind is fortunately and unfortunately given by our basic disposition, our neurophysiological substratum. In the course of the phylogenetic development of animals, those organs which ceased to be functional gradually disappeared (gills, for instance, metamorphosed into lungs), whereas in humans the ancient tribal "animal" brain survives basically unchanged as the center directing the vital functions and ensuring the coordinated functioning of the organism, and as the seat of instinct, enabling individual survival and the continuation of the human race altogether. This unchanged brain gives birth to primal aggressions. From the distant past relics of tribal feeling emerge, but at the same time the sexual and feeding urge and the maternal instinct emerge, and here too is the source of artistic creativity. The weeping of Bosnian mothers and the hatred of the gunmen spring from the same source, however much the intentions and value systems of the two groups may be in opposition to each other.

This tribal brain is covered only by a thin, two-to-five-millimeter layer of the cerebral cortex. Grey brain matter: the immensely fragile seat of proud humanity, a trifle which has made possible the greatest achievements of the spirit, the creative and refuting mouth that has eaten enthusiastically of the tree of knowledge and has many times endured dyspepsia from that food...

And only in the mutual interaction of these brains, to express it simply, is a space of various levels created for a balanced, integrated humanity. This vision of humanity is evidently the most difficult task of human history, as it has never yet been accomplished...

The striking failures of the noble conceptions of all the idealistic moralists and advocates of human brotherhood and tolerance are undoubtedly due to this fact: these humanists, in their schematic dualities of good and evil, did not give sufficient emphasis to that other, dark and instinctive brain, the one they wished to exclude from the game. Today we can still hear the desperate voices of Erasmus and Comenius over history, we can still see the closed eyes of Tolstoy's illusions, we still regret the pacifist vanities of wanting to erase all wars, without giving that dark brain alternative nourishment... More and more we become aware of the kind of inherited, innate weaknesses of the splendid Utopian projects of the Platos, Mores, Campanellas and Saint-Simons. And we are (rightfully) distrustful of anything of that sort, when we reflect on what monstrosities were perpetrated by those who claimed that these noble men were their still "naive" predecessors. The sun that rises over such a state usually sets only over barracks and labor camps...

Those very people who were the advocates and originators of violence and intolerance were always well aware of that darkness in humankind, and knew how to work purposefully with that world of instinct and how to navigate it. That too is why their intellectual organizations of violence and their destructive passions have always been "more mature" and "more effective" in practice than any kind of abstract model which, with refer-

ence to sovereign human reason, has ever been offered by
the humanist spirits throughout time. The humanists mostly
preached to the converted, and their sorrowful weeping over
constant defeats had the alluring flavor of masochism for the
sadistic bearers of power; the badly needed drugs that only increased the delight of the orgiastic ravings...

Himmler's perfectly organized death machines are more than
convincing proof of how well the gray brain matter knows how to
serve the dark instincts, how mechanistic reason and irrational-
ity can suit one another. The brain easily finds justification for
demons; its perfection of them is methodical. The creativity of
intolerance is almost admirable only because of the inventive-
ness of reason, which arrogantly surpasses all limits of humanity, up to superman and down below the animals at the same
time.

So the whole problem of the humanization of history may lie
in whether anyone will ever succeed in reversing these tendencies, whether at some time the subcortical will begin to serve
sovereign reason, and whether at the same time reason will acknowledge its own limits. Another vain Utopia?

We already know, for example from Dostoyevsky, how profoundly and indivisibly our "higher" and "lower" psychic structures are interconnected. It has also been empirically proven by
stereotactic tests on the brain, which can be ordered by the court
in some countries in the case of a particularly dangerous criminal. It is indeed possible with a surgical operation to eliminate
the biological center of undesired aggressiveness, but thus far
not without changing the entire personality, without violating
its integrity and identity. Such measures then verge on psychic
murder...

We are living in a world in which evidently the level of tolerance
is rising – as well as that of intolerance. Unfortunately in the
least desirable direction. First of all *tolerance of intolerance* is
growing. The television screen brings pictures of violence, sad-
ism and cruel repression of all kinds into our homes between the
armchair and the baby crib as something ordinary, normal and

everyday. These pictures, in which the horrible details of muti-
lated bodies are shown from flattering angles, evoke a rather su-
praliminal inhibition, or else they become subliminal, so that
the result is often mere apathy. As if a kind of "fateful modus"
were lacking, at every moment everything is at stake, but unfortunately somehow at every moment it is enough to turn one's
head away and then it seems that nothing is at stake...

I am not thinking only of live reportage of war and the taste
of jouralists for the sharp flavor of blood and death, but still
more of the flood of action films, in which evil armed with might
is presented as attractive, offers itself for imitation and is imi-
tated. Extreme states of the human psyche, such as the ruthless
and disintegrated brutality of psychopaths, are becoming attractive. This phenomenon represents a risky, foolhardy experimentation in the liquid sands of the human psyche. Again the gray
matter of the brain serves the dark instincts, this time in the
interests of profit. So far we are playing with released jinns, but
soon they will start playing with us.

The *intolerance of tolerance* is growing too. Tolerance is still
more or less put up with (if only as a peculiar and impractical
character trait) but as soon as it is presented as a general value
and desirable norm it usually arouses distaste; yes, even disgust. Not only is tolerance regarded as unrealistic, a fairy-tale
illusion, something absurd – it is even *a limine* suspected of hypocrisy, weakness, cowardice...

The sober voice of the historian can certainly try to stop such
lamentations with a pointed reference to the episodes of repeated intolerance in history, which have alternated with only brief
periods of real tolerance.

Of course it is possible to object that crisis periods such as
today's (in the history of culture, our era is connected with the
Mannerist period) have been augurs of global catastrophe – the
fall of the Roman Empire, the Thirty Years' War, World War I.
And today there are several additional horrifying symptoms of
crisis. Roughly until the end of the 19th century, "evil was indeed done, but good was respected" as Ortega concluded. The
present day in many of its manifestations does not even delay
itself with this hypocrisy; death cults, xenophobic groups, sa-

tanists of various denominations may be mentioned here as *pars pro toto*. Along with the appearance of many expressions of elementary disrespect for life (from maltreatment of children, the sick and animals, to army bullying and motiveless cruel murders, up to ethnic genocide) the very instinct of self-preservation is breaking down alarmingly. The anarchist terrorist used to hurl his bomb at his victims and then tried to save his own life by running for shelter, but many terrorists today are prepared, as a matter of course, to die with their victims. This is a dangerous novelty. The question as to whether it is not a case of multiple suicide can easily, with the chronic shortage of defensive materials, become an existential question for the future of the whole of humankind. Pushkin's words, "For the Russian, his own life is worth half a kopek; another's is worth nothing at all!" do not only apply to the Russians of his time...

As is evident from its etymology, tolerance has always been connected with sacrifice, with self-acceptance, self-mastery, with a certain self-restriction. Tolerance is connected with all those traits that we have become accustomed, in the European tradition, to consider as *cultural*. Even in the animal world there exists a unique phenomenon that seems to be the embryonic state of the link between culture and tolerance. From time immemorial dolphins have rescued drowing people, especially children. They saved them despite the fact that dolphins have an easily vulnerable body surface and therefore "man hurts them." Culture and tolerance also "hurt," yet they exist "despite" that fact – and only thanks to that "violence" against animal "naturalness" do they exist at all, forming a second, higher naturalness.

What should one rely on? Appeals to reason evidently do not help; emotions often only increase the pressure in the overheated boiler. So perhaps force? As is evident in various locations, military force can perhaps ensure a conditional and limited truce, but due to its own repressive nature it cannot revive the mechanism for tolerance or abolish fundamental paranoiac mutual distrust, the roots of which are hidden in the remote past of history. (The borders of the Balkan conflict, for instance, are practically identical to the borders of the Eastern and Western Roman Empire and to the frontiers of the ecclesiastical schism in the 11th century!)

It is hard to blame manipulated ethnic Narcissists for submitting, in the furious whirlwind of the battle of everyone against everyone, to the incredible squandering of human and material resources right down to the bottom. Their heads are lost in headless multi-headedness. They will not get any antidotes from within themselves. These were provided over the centuries by culture, philosophy and religion. Specialized sciences have ousted philosophy from its sovereign throne (Wittgenstein: "All that is left to philosophy is analysis of language"); religion for the most part preaches to the converted.

And culture? And literature?

F. X. Šalda once, almost unwittingly, said the main thing: "Culture begins with a sense of nuances and ends with a sense of mutuality and wholeness." This sentence can also define the territory of tolerance. Respect for nuances is an expression of respect for the unique, for individuality, for the exception. But this respect in the absolute can lead to a cult of the special, the extreme. On the other hand, an isolated sense of "wholeness," neglecting inner differentiations, leads to the formation of rigid, "pure" systems, to intolerant authoritativeness... So they must both apply...

Julien Benda, in his famous *Trahison des Clercs,* prophetically named the magical attraction of power for intellectuals, who voluntarily renounce their responsibility to critically and impartially reflect the state of the world. He analyzed the mechanisms by which intellectuals cease to be internally-directed individuals and start to participate in their own depersonalization, making themselves into servants; they cease unconsciously or conscious-

ly to see themselves. Warning is useless. After the experience of
so many cases of intellectual hara-kiri in the great totalitarian
systems of our age, culture has, as if in self-defense, renounced
any possible intervention in world events. It has become "marginal" and has accepted this "marginality" humbly for itself: it
has collapsed into itself, into its own internal codes. The vertical
cult of universality has been replaced by the horizontal cult of
hodgepodge, the post-modernist currency: "the edge is everywhere, the center nowhere." It is as if it were a conscious denial
of the Aristotelian definition of God's world: "The center is everywhere, the edge nowhere." The reflection of history as a meaningful motion is replaced by the palimpsest transparencies, dis-
interested in values, of heterogeneous cultural zones, consisting
of secondary interpretations that make a blasé, scornful gesture
of victory over the search for and expression of the primary, for
"there are no final truths." The authentic is replaced by mere
singularity and its noncommittal personal myths, which alone
guarantee (to themselves) their credibility and the impossibility
of their misuse in false collective myths.

Culture voluntarily locked between the prefixes *de-* and *post-*
thus clears a space, which is immediately occupied by dema-
gogues and all kinds of specialized manipulators. Often they
themselves become the judges of their methods, with the help of
pictures and codes which culture and especially literature created in their myth-forming past.

It would seem, of course, that this freed-up horizontal current, this market of ideas, in itself creates tolerance, in the same
way that it is allegedly created by advertising. But tolerance, in
an era in which anything is replaceable by anything, becomes
boundless and internally noncommittal. Tolerance worth nothing. Tolerance with the current switched off.

Not only books by the great humanists, but also practical experiences often convince us that tolerance, provided it does not
come from Šalda's "sense of mutuality and wholeness" and is not
conditioned by the knowledge of higher unities and does not
refer to them, easily ends in intolerance. We can unfortunately

observe the dominance of partial approaches in many organizations that want to promote their varied interests in a free, plu-
ralistic society, including those which are certainly praiseworthy
and legal. The absolutist approach to particularities, biting its
own tail, deafened by egocentric hubbub, makes its cause too
vulnerable by isolating it – and (perhaps unconsciously) thus
makes it easy and tasty bait for advocates of the "firm hand" of
totalitarian unified norms. If we observe these intolerant tolerant people, fanatics of "their truth," we often feel that they do
not want to be bound up by the law they insist on, but only that
through tenacious struggle for their order, for their inner truth,
they unleash themselves; they *want* to unleash themselves.

So that again it is not a matter of tolerance as an essential
"bearing from the fundamental." The path to the tolerant "me
and you" on the contrary turns back to the paranoid animosity of
"us and them"...

After all, in the comprehension of tolerance in general, the liber-
alist pragmatic approach, founded on "functional concessions,"
prevails: "If you concede to me here, I will in return give way to
you elsewhere, in something else." This benevolence of mutual
advantage engenders a feeling of the decency of democratic con-
sensus. It is considered a sufficiently good, desirable and indeed
ideal state of affairs. The correlation with market principles is
evident here, but market logic does not go beyond the principle
of "an eye for an eye, a tooth for a tooth" either...

Such a state of affairs, a state of agreements which are not
after all crafty and are in principle adhered to, is rightly taken
as honorable, if only because it can include the codified principle
of surrendering claim to those personal rights that could harm
the other side. But from the aspect of higher and fundamental
norms (tolerance as "to bear from the fundamental"), it seems
inadequate. For such a conditional state gives no guarantees,
such as can emerge only from something that is unconditional.
The contract expires, and if its conditions do not suit me any
longer, I shall not renew it, nor perhaps the temporary tolerance
that went with it. That is the tolerance of the small-minded from

which egocentric, cowardly and infamous appeasements of all kinds are born. This is really only about "defining a territory of interests," with which humankind only slightly elevates itself above the level of marking out frontiers by smell, as higher mammals do. At times when the game of interests becomes a game of existence or nonexistence, tolerance is of course valuable and gratefully accepted. That gratitude, that relief we all feel if there is at least some kind of expression of tolerance, particularly if it is bound by a contract, should not of course lull us and blind us to higher possibilities.

How much more exalted, deeper and stronger tolerance would be if, for instance, we could say to one another: we have met on holy ground. It is the ground of our Earth and our lives. Earth and lives that we have not created ourselves, so that we are not masters here, but only temporary administrators. Therefore and in the name of the temporary ownership of these gifts, let us agree like the ambassadors of distant kings, who in us and through us show respect and express love. Such a reconsecration of the violated territory of life, its new sanctification, is perhaps the only thing that could still save our civilization in the twilight of the millennium from destruction. That is the distance that forms true nearness, nearness through the general, universal, through the paramount.

The sources for such a turn towards the renewal of the earth, the renewal of the cosmic and timeless status of humankind, are still here, however buried, however nearly invisible. Theologians often remind us that God "speaks softly" within us, and they write of the difficulty of distinguishing the color of God's voice among many voices. The loudest is always the voice of one's imperative self. Therefore we must be quiet, so that we can hear the other voice and with it all human voices from the beginning of time. Inquisitive mutual goodwill is only the first condition; the second, more basic one is an acceptance of one's own imperfection, which depends on chance and is a fundamental condition for growth. "To bear one's burden from the fundamental" means also to bear the other human being, not drag him or her into the hatred that I feel for myself. Creative self-love lays down a positive basis and chronic lack of it makes it impossible

to understand and act upon the very difficult demand of the
fundamental commandment of Christianity: "Thou shalt love
thy neighbour *as thyself.*"

I know of no deeper and more verifiable condition of true tolerance which is not just a virtue of necessity. I know of no more
essential foundation for "love of strangers" which is not just sly
hypocrisy and a self-important empty gesture.

RUDOLF MATYS (1938)
Poet and essayist
Prague

Daniela Fischerová

THE MASSAGE TABLE

WHO IS WHO, WHAT IS WHAT:

The DEVIL wears a naive St. Nicholas' Day devil mask, according to Czech traditions. The DEVIL's companions do not perceive him on the stage. He comes across as hearty and jovial.

The MASSEUR is a sturdy, completely shaven young man. On his chest is tattooed *The Scourge of God*. On his body are pictures of a ruder nature. He wears a hearing aid and speaks with the loud voice of the deaf. Peculiar.

The WOMAN is middle-aged, unkempt. She reaches towards her aching head and moans. She appears at the end of her strength.

LUSTRACE is a screening process for identifying former agents of the STB, the state secret police, as well as members of the People's Militia and high-ranking Communist officials. In 1991 in Czechoslovakia many people received notification of their "positive lustrace," which barred them from working in any government or state institution for 5 years (until 1996). But there quickly appeared many forgeries, which people sent out of vengeance and malice.

The massage table. Under it the DEVIL is lounging. A huge spider dangles from his fingers. The MASSEUR is sitting on the table, apathetically lashing himself. There is a knock. The MASSEUR doesn't react. The DEVIL expectantly watches. Another knock. The DEVIL sticks the spider in his mouth and chews. After the third knock the WOMAN enters. She doesn't see the DEVIL.

DEVIL *(sweetly)*: It wasn't real. But it looked real. A comical
prop. That's really my brand of humor.

*He victoriously spits out the spider. The WOMAN is confused.
Alarmed, she watches the MASSEUR's flagellations. She enters
into his field of vision.*

MASSEUR *(rudely)*: You don't have an appointment. My shift's
over.
WOMAN: My god, help me. I can't fall sleep. I haven't slept for
a week!
DEVIL: Big deal. I never sleep. So what?
MASSEUR *(Puts in his hearing aid)*: What did you say? You
have to speak loudly.
WOMAN: I can't sleep. I can't sleep! It's like there's a kicked-in
anthill in my head. You're my last hope. If I don't fall asleep
immediately, I'll go crazy. *(Shouts)* I'll go crazy!
MASSEUR *(With a sigh)*: All right. So get undressed.
WOMAN *(Pointing at his chest)*: What have you got here?
MASSEUR: It's from prison.
WOMAN: Oh. *(She undresses, with anxiety)* What are you going
to do with me?
MASSEUR: Cast the devil out of you. Go on!

The DEVIL snickers. Frightened, the WOMAN stops undressing.

WOMAN: They told me you're a masseur.
MASSEUR *(Moving his fingers)*: It tingles. It always tingles
when the devil's around. I can feel Evil here.
WOMAN *(shrinking back)*: But... I'm a nonbeliever.
DEVIL: In what?
WOMAN *(She thinks that the MASSEUR spoke)*: What do you
mean "in what?"
DEVIL: In what don't you believe? In evil?
WOMAN: In anything. That's the horrible part, I don't believe
in anything anymore.

*The DEVIL blows her a kiss. The WOMAN collapses in the chair,
despairingly.*

WOMAN: Do what you want with me. Just make me fall
asleep.

*She closes her eyes. The MASSEUR takes out his hearing aid. With
fingers tensed he moves around the WOMAN's body, mumbling to
himself. His fingers begin to wiggle. Magically they're drawn
under the table. The DEVIL nonchalantly deflects the MASSEUR's
gesture.*

WOMAN: How old are you? You remind me of my son. He's also
sort of a... baldy. Shaved to the scalp like a billiard ball. He
looks like a baby. He used to be really nice, a wonderful
child. Now, he paints swastikas here. *(She taps on the top of
her skull, groans)* Ow!
MASSEUR: *(Searching. Mumbles)*: Evil, Evil... I'll find it... I
feel it here...
DEVIL: Bravo, bravo! Is that a man, or what? Searching for
evil is a very laudable hobby. At the very least, we highly
recommend it. And we always get what we want anyway.
WOMAN: He was also locked up. But not because of his beliefs,
like you. He stole a car. *(She climbs half-naked onto the
table.)* From that time on he's been a bad kid. They must
have hurt him there. He's gone bad.

*A piece of paper falls out of her clothes. The WOMAN isn't aware
of anything. Lying down, the DEVIL places it into the fumbling
hand of the MASSEUR and blows a joyful fanfare.*

DEVIL: Attention one and all. A devilish joke's about to fall.
WOMAN *(miserably)*: He lost a finger there. People say they
stuck his hand into a vice. Do you think it's possible? Is it
really that horrible there –
MASSEUR *(Holding up the paper, ecstatically)*: Evil! I found it.
Evil!
WOMAN *(frantically)*: Gimmee that!

*She jumps off the table, trying to take the piece of paper from
him. The MASSEUR pushes her away. The DEVIL enthusiastically
whistles like a referee for a fight.*

MASSEUR *(Enunciating carefully, because of the difficulty of
the text):* Notification of the result of the *lustrace*. Result is
POSITIVE! So that's why you're not sleeping!

WOMAN: But it's not true!

MASSEUR *(ecstatically)*: No evil remains hidden from the eyes
of God.

WOMAN: It's a mistake! It's –

MASSEUR *(ecstatically)*: Get on the table!

WOMAN: I never had any contact with them in my life –

MASSEUR: On the table!!!

WOMAN: I know you had your own suffering.... You're so
suspicious... all of you. My son too... To you everyone is
suddenly some kind of bastard, but I never –

*He grabs hold of her and puts her on the table. With his back to
her he moves his fingers to warm them up. Terrified, the WOMAN
watches with her eyes wide open. Then she carefully climbs down
from the table and whispers to the MASSEUR's back:*

WOMAN: Hey! Hey! *(Collects her clothes, quietly)* Boo!

DEVIL *(Exaggeratedly looking up towards heaven)*: Lord!
Adonai! *(Listens for a moment, comtemplating.)* Nothing.
Deaf as a post. "Vanity of vanities; all is vanity." My
favorite quotation. I'll write it in all the girls' yearbooks. A
flash of healthy reason from the Bible, don't you think? I
would also gladly write the slogan, "The end justifies the
means."

*The WOMAN steals away. The DEVIL sticks his leg out from under
the table. The WOMAN trips and falls.*

WOMAN *(Horrified)*: You have no right to judge me! You have
no –

The MASSEUR turns around and looks at her with a peculiar indifference. Trembling, she returns to the table as if hypnotized.

DEVIL: I wonder what she'll say, huh? I'll bet it'll be the typically emotional barrage of unbelievably poor excuses: I had no idea, oh. They forced me, always. Let him who is without sin cast the first stone. Before the conclusion, I propose a theological interlude. Saint Francis maintains that we all come in pairs. The sinner and the saint, who derives pleasure from his damnation. A very promising motif. – Wait, she's about to speak. I'm really curious.

WOMAN *(Shouts out with despair)*: Just so you know, I'd do it again.

The DEVIL applauds. The WOMAN is horrified at what she just said. Then she realizes that the MASSEUR doesn't hear her. She begins calmly, and gradually works herself into a frenzy.

WOMAN: Who gave you the right to judge us? Who? Who do you think you are? Just because you suffered, you can destroy us? Everyone's afraid of you now just like they were afraid of the others before! Only you are worse. At least they knew they were assholes, and got a kick out of it. Whereas you don't even know who you are!

DEVIL *(Cheerfully)*: Bravo. Francis, I'll take them both!

WOMAN: You mean you're looking for evil? You and your shaved head? But it's written in your eyes — You don't want justice. You just want revenge.

MASSEUR *(inserting his hearing aid)*: Did you say something? When I take it out, I'm as deaf as a post.

WOMAN *(immediately losing courage, confused)*: No, no... I only... You always had... this... foresight... ?

MASSEUR *(shakes his head)*: I sinned and repented and God forgave me.

WOMAN: Repent, repent... Am I supposed to repent too or what? And before whom? Before him? He doesn't want me to repent. He wants me to drop dead!

MASSEUR: He wants us to repent. Without repentance there's

no forgiveness, and without forgiveness, there's no
salvation.

WOMAN *(furiously)*: I'm not talking about God! I'm talking
about my son! When he found the letter, he smeared shit on
all the doorknobs. Do you know what he said before he ran
away from home? Informers and Gypsies to the gas
chamber! That's what you've made out of us! Everybody
hates someone! This one hates Gypsies, that one
Communists! This one hates hairy people, that one hairless.
Some people hate Jews and everybody altogether hates
secret police agents.

MASSEUR *(Takes out his hearing aid, aloof)*: On the table.

*The WOMAN rushes at him and beats him with her fists. He
stands there, silent.*

WOMAN: Jesus, stick that goddamn hearing aid in there! How
am I supposed to defend myself when you don't even listen
to me? You Scourge of God or whatever the hell you've
cracked yourself up to be! You prophetic martyr! As for my
being some kind of agent? No! *(He stares at her fixedly. She
confesses.)* I had to go there! But I always just cried and
told them: I don't know, I don't know, I don't know
anything. *(She adds.)* I never informed on anyone. *(She
adds.)* Only a little bit. *(She collapses, blubbering.)* What
could I do? After all, they told me that otherwise my boy
would never come home alive.

MASSEUR *(Puts his hearing aid back in)*: You talk too much.
I'm not going to massage you like this.

WOMAN *(In tears, pathetically)*: I want to repent! Am I
supposed to kneel in the corner until I die? But how, how?
Tell me how! *(He shrugs his shoulders.)* How can it be you
don't know? And who's supposed to know anyway? After all,
they put you away because of your beliefs!

MASSEUR: It wasn't because of my beliefs.

WOMAN: Then why?

MASSEUR *(Expressionless)*: I strangled my wife.

The WOMAN is in shock. The MASSEUR takes her to the table, removes his hearing aid, and makes a gesture indicating strangulation. The WOMAN closes her eyes in horror, but he starts massaging her neck. She groans from the pain.

MASSEUR *(Sings out of tune, loudly, but with a certain command or air):*
    I flee to Your bosom, that I may not be ashamed for
                              eternity,
    For before Your memory, who could endure? Who?

The DEVIL has another big spider dangling from his fingers. He is playing with it.

DEVIL: You dear little imp, I say to myself. What's the secret of your power? Fools say: lies. No, no! That's a verisimilitude. I am the little white lie in which there's still a little truth, I am the truth in which there's a little white lie, a fascinating mishmash of lies and truth, much more effective than any pure lie.
WOMAN: For God's sake, let me sleep... just let me sleep!
DEVIL: Put a teaspoon of poison into a barrel of honey, and the result is a barrel of poison. Drop a teaspoon of honey into a barrel of poison and, what do you know – the result is poison again! We don't need much. The greatest advantage of Evil is economy.
MASSEUR: My guilt, my guilt, my guilt!
    To be forgiven, in tears I confess my guilt.
DEVIL *(Eats the spider)*: It was real. But you all think it's just a prop, that it was a so-called devilish trick. The creation of illusion we entrust to Disneyland. Our business is to affirm that nothing is real.

The MASSEUR finishes the massage. The WOMAN blows her nose, gets dressed.

WOMAN *(Desperately)*: Is that all? I'm worse than before. *(She looks in the mirror)* My eyes are all puffy and bloodshot.

Soon there'll be sulphuric acid running out of me. I set all
my hopes on you. On a common murderer. It's fraud,
everthing. The amnesty too! They should have kept him
there. Nobody should've ever forgiven anybody for anything.
DEVIL: Allow me to unmask myself. My big moment has come!

*He removes the devil mask and bows. He crawls out from under
the table and collides with the woman. He angrily waves the piece
of paper.*

DEVIL: I hear they sent this to you! This trash! This crap!
WOMAN: What?
DEVIL: Isn't it clear to you that it's a forgery? This was sent
   by some asshole who wanted to set us against each other.
WOMAN *(Collapses in the chair, astounded)*: So it's not real?
DEVIL: Oh come now! You, an informer? Such a respectable
   lady? Definitely not you! But look what I've got here! *(He
   waves a fan of similar papers.)* Clean, unsigned, all ready to
   be filled in! Send them to whomever you like! Just out of
   revenge! And a lot of people would deserve it anyway! I
   believe it's our moral duty to do it! Are we supposed to let
   the fucking agents get away, just like that? Come on, take a
   few! You've certainly got someone to send it to! And didn't
   they hurt you terribly, after all? They corrupted your boy!
   You can't even sleep! Yeah!

*The WOMAN stares at the papers the whole time as if bewitched by
the thought. She reaches out for them with her hand, waging an
internal struggle. The DEVIL winks at the audience.*

WOMAN: No... not that. I can't do it. It's sick and disgusting.
   Yech.

*She withdraws her hand and immediately falls asleep like a log.
The DEVIL disappointedly shakes his head. He puts his mask on
again, giving in. The MASSEUR sits on the table, commences
whipping himself and mumbles his psalm.*

DEVIL: Nay, hang it up, imp. "A minion of that force am I
which would/Do evil foul yet in the end do good." "Vanity of
vanities; all is vanity." *Vanitas vanitatum et omnia vanitas.*
(Starts off, turns once more.) I even know it in Hebrew.
Havel havalim, havel havalim, hakol havel.

*The DEVIL disappears. The woman snores. The masseur's pecu-
liar singing is heard.*

DANIELA FISCHEROVÁ (1948)
Dramatist and novelist
Prague

Miroslav Holub

NOT SO SUCCINCT REFLECTIONS ON AN EDICT

An edict, evidently Diocletian,
posted in the year 201 in the marketplace of Aizanoi,
sets down in stone:

Man aged 16–40 .... 30,000 denarii
Woman of same age .... 25,000 denarii
Homo ab annis LX superius et VIII inferius ...... 15,000 denarii
Mulier – i.e. a woman – aetatis   –"–   .... 10,000 denarii
Riding horse.. 100,000 denarii
Equus militaris primae formae .... 36,000 denarii
Dromedarius optimus .... 20,000 denarii
Vacca – i.e. cow – formae primae .... 2,000 denarii
Capra – i.e. goat – formae primae......................... 600 denarii

Those are certainly accommodating prices.
For one army horse, three girls aged up to eight years
and ten good goats isn't much at all.
Besides, who knows how the girls will grow up?

For two men in their productive years
you can get as many as three dromedaries,
whose nutritional needs are far less demanding,
because in need they can drink their own piss.

And who today would offer almost seven old men
for a dappled riding horse?
Possibly Richard III, but
that was ages ago.

For a contract on a creditor you'd pay today
less than for a Mercedes 230,
for a football player primae formae
let's say a pound of gold, which was 72,000 denarii,

but he would have to be a spy, so that
for his head the secret service would pay the price of
eight little lads in basic school
or a herd of Phrygian cows of Frisian pedigree.

A herd of little girls earns in one month on the street
only enough for a two-humped camel,
which was 60,000... Whatever, Diocletian prices
were accommodating, but mainly they existed, period.

It is, of course, revolting to sell slaves on the market;
even if here and there the ground swells up and yields
                                                    thousands
of priceless yellow, black and white bloody heads,
kwashiorkor bellies like rosary beads,

leading to the absolute of celestial canteens,
as if from coiled, vitreous pupae
climbing one finger at a time with crumpled nails,
like herpetic sphinxes, irreversible hands,

groping over the plains, where armless
philosophers graze cotton swabs,
thinking less about blood
than about cellulose.

The hands grope and clench
and turn to jelly in a final pull
when no one is up to philosophy any more,
nor the emperor, nor ice cream.

It is, of course, revolting to sell slaves on the market,
even if a rabid poet is calling out his prices
for dextrorotatory metaphysical mussels,
for a serpent's pensive overcoat

veiling tepid vulcan depths
in which even the pubic bone would expire,
even if the poet is dreaming of self-procreating genitals
strewn in the bush like ascomycetes.

Then poetry calls to mind
one hundred fifty eyes of cats,
pickled in vinegar so that
immortality can be seen.

It is, of course, revolting to sell slaves on the market
when nowadays even spirochetes are memorizing
the act of habeas corpus and man is reaching to the stars
and to black holes as early as the gastrulic stage.

It is, of course, revolting to sell slaves on the market;
even if the value of man is not known,
even if the value of each particular man,
even if the value,
even if the man...

Oh yes, Diocletian.
This edict is still valid to a degree,
on one hand partially in practice,
on the other, partially in the so-called soul.

MIROSLAV HOLUB (1932)
Poet and immunologist
Prague

CLASS IN
SESSION IN B.

"Children," the teacher begins. He clears his throat, stares cross-eyed at a piece of paper half-shielded by his hand on the desk-top, and announces: "We are not going to learn for now. We are going to talk and play." In the lesson plan, which he had spent half the night writing, only to end up summarizing everything he had crossed out on one-eighth of a sheet of paper, he reads the note: Playschool – dist. teacher's conf. (Comenius & Pesta-lozzi). Clear methodological instructions. It only becomes a prob-lem when he finds himself face to face with the class in connec-tion with the topic chosen by vote at that same teachers' confer-ence. He has summed it up in one single word, albeit one which evokes respect, the most impressive word when written: TOL-ERANCE.

And now he is supposed to explain this to a bunch of lanky ten-year-olds, whose fathers – if they are lucky – work in the port nearby loading hundreds of tons of freight every day while their buddies yell: "Fuck ya mutha!" – or maybe they're firing off mortars just a few hundred miles away from here to that same yell. But he must make the same point to the diminutive sons and daughters of "Little Indochina," the immigrant colony down by the Rhine, as well as to those fidgety Sicilians, Moroccans, Turks, Kurds and Albanians who open their mouths only during clashes over language and who when alone remain proudly si-lent (including, as a rule, whenever the teacher asks a question).

Not counting himself, from two nations by origin, like a size-able number of the locals these days, the only kindred Swiss in the class are the Huber twins, Carmen and Mercedes, daughters of a Swiss single mother who has given up hope that her fiancé and the girls' father, repatriated to the faraway Santiago de Chile after years in exile, will ever return. Both the half-Swiss girls, however, are openly proud of possessing this elite citizen-

ship in a worker's district and country where the heavy labor is
performed almost exclusively by foreigners. And they consider it
both their right and their responsibility to check the papers of
their non-citizen classmates with no less rigor than the federal
and canton police check their parents'.

At this very moment one of the twins, following whispered
consultations with her sister, is frantically demanding that she
be called on, while the teacher, having learned from experience,
is looking the other way. He has no desire to investigate affairs
such as: "Mladenović ate my lunch and stuck a rubber in my bag,
like the kind you get AIDS from. Should I go to the doctor?" That
particular investigation dragged on for over an hour and produced no conclusions other than that there was indeed a pack of
condoms in one of the Hubers' bags. However, the box had not
been opened and resembled the ones that representatives of the
federal health administration had been passing out in the
schoolyard that same day as part of a new program called "Pre-
vention Starts with Contraception."

Whoever was to blame for the whole prank, whether it was
theft, mistaken identity, or an act of provocation, was, it goes
without saying, left uninvestigated. So the teacher ignores little
Carmen from the Rhine and instead gives the nod to Antonio,
the lively Sicilian, the only one of the little islanders exhibiting
a willingness to break the scout's vow of silence. Antonio leaps
from his chair and gushes with delight:

"You sayed, I heared, we gonna talk. So I say – I talk – with
that boo... bomb? Like time there was splosion in Palermo. And
there was a lots of splosions, and Uncle Salvatore, he was there,
but no morte... he shood... lui spara... I mean like if when someone wants shoo someone... and he shood there too..."

At which point one of his countrymen explodes out of his chair
like a bomb: "Taci, traditore. Chiudi il becco!"

The teacher, who at one time studied his country's third language because he was required to, understands enough to know
the traitor has been emphatically requested to shut his trap. As
an educator he can only pretend that he either hasn't heard or
hasn't understood. For which of his great model educators would
advise him to get mixed up in the disputes of foreigners whose

mentality he understands even less than their language? On top
of that, in the modern age of migration of nations throughout
the world, of wars afflicting even this continent, of rampant
crime afflicting mainly the young and even children – the ones
he is supposed to be instilling with tolerance?

To be sure, Comenius brought his life's work to completion in
a foreign land, and that was at the time of the Thirty Years' War,
whose brutality took away a homeland from him and all hope
from his nation. And yet it didn't take away his faith in better-
ment. But is the uncertain voice of the heart armament enough
for a teacher who is, after all, no priest, and who, in the labyrinth of today's world is threatened by – the word was unknown
in their day – the mafia? Or is it only a modern form of the age-
old lack of faith that blinds us and enfeebles us from the very
start: the word? And with which word to begin a discourse on the
need for love and hope in a world that lacks tolerance?

The classroom rustles with quiet commotion among the desks,
and the teacher gazes absently out the open window at the honey haze of Indian summer that hangs over the surface of the
river, tinted with color by the nearby chemical labs. Behind his
back, pushing and shoving, muffled cries in several tongues, a
conflict of passions still childlike, though far beyond the age of
innocence. The tug-of-war over the borders staked out in the
classroom – invisibly yet audibly, according either to language or
to accent alone – drowns out for a moment the helicopter land-
ing on the level roof of the hospital. All at once the teacher gets
an idea worthy of either of his illustrious countrymen and educational models: as if Jan Amos, countryman on his father's side,
and Johann Heinrich, of his maternal nation, were nodding to
him from the clouds outside the window exuding the faint odor
of gasoline vapor.

"Children," the teacher turns to his pupils, some of them still
engaged in the never-ending class struggle, "put on your things.
We're going to the Rhine."

You can't step twice into the same river. Today that river is baby-pink, yolk-yellow and moss-green, foaming over with the incoming tide in a special blend produced by the neighboring dye and pharmaceuticals operations, among the world leaders in their field. Additional proof of their quality is the speed with which their chemical researchers managed to clean up the waters of the Rhine after contaminating it with their own poisons in that well-known catastrophe, now rightfully forgotten.

After all, those surface colors, lending the zip and glamor of a theater premiere to autumn in these parts, have ceased to be a hazard to life and will be captured just a ways downstream by the new, efficient purifiers. For that matter, the fish are back living in the river, some, they say, of previously unseen shapes and colors.

This reappearance of life as well as this evidence of his people's diligence brings joy to the maternal spirit of the soul of teacher Jan Pražák, addressed by his pupils in the neighborly traditions of universal democracy and dialectic phonetics as Mr. Pracák. That unpronounceable little hook over the "z" is, to be sure, no less deeply lodged in the emotional store of the youthful teacher – like his father, an impassioned historian, chess player and fisherman – than the apothecary's precision of his mother's family, the Pfisters, with whose members he shares a sensitivity to weight (of words), moderation (of things) and value (of deeds).

As a Czech patriot, he tells the children what he learned from his father about the death of Jan Hus by fire on the banks of the Rhine, near the town of Kostnice, where in modern times they not only established a museum to the martyr, but have now even named a bistro after him. Less than an hour's ride away by car, in fact, following the footsteps of the Hussite delegation, which doubtless proceeded along the Rhine to the negotiations in this very place, in ancient Basle, whose parlors and workplaces today play host to many a countryman and countrywoman on their traditional pilgrimages from the Czech lands to the end of the world. Many of them got no farther, bound for good by the Rhine metropolis, this ageless attractor of refugees and adventurers, of thinkers, artists and also lunatics; from Erasmus Rotterdam to

Bohuslav Martinů, from Huguenot silk merchants and mechanics of the Czech Brethren to researchers in genetics, whose brains matter more than where they come from.

As a Swiss settler, the teacher Pražák-Pfister, in the spirit of his family tree, directs the movement of nations since time immemorial into a line of pupils marching toward the desired educational goal: the peaceful border of three states within the flow of a single river!

A clear case of tolerance in practice, and perhaps also a convincing one for the children, who have here neither roots nor a future: their fathers are selected for the permitted contingent of arrivals to do only that work which even the local unemployed either do not want or cannot perform.

While this flow over frontiers is certainly not unique in history, chroniclers by and large record the visits of prominent personalities rather than the march or even the stampede of the masses – in pursuit of bread, out of shooting range, in pursuit of illusions of a better future. In pursuit of teaching, never!

So Pražák's kids, too, freed for the moment from the obligation to sit still and listen to a wearying sermon in a foreign tongue on the meaning of a democracy no less foreign to most of them, chase after freedom as they see fit: the Sicilians sprint off in pursuit of Antonio the traitor, who is so far successfully maintaining his head start; the mixed Arab gang is badgering the squealing Alpine-Andean Huber girls with something on the end of a stick that strongly resembles the subject of the recent investigation; meanwhile, the Balkan Slavs are mixing it up homestyle among themselves, and with the Albanians and the Turks, while the Kurds of course lurk in the background, waiting for the Turks to show a moment of weakness. A few West Europeans and the class's lone Pole are the only ones who do not use force to solve their disputes, detouring widely around the scufflers, their hushed pronouncements punctuated by numbers.

So deeply are they immersed in their number-crunching debate, however, that they pay no attention to their surroundings. And so it is that when the teacher comes to a stop finally to point out the now visible goal – a triple frontier in the form of a silvery pillar, sunk into the riverbed of the Rhine like a rocket – the only one listening is Ljubica, a Serbian girl, who seizes the situation to rescue herself from the onslaught of her Croatian classmates. The teacher is, however, accustomed to the Babylonian confusion, and cannot be prevented by this petty disturbance from proceeding according to his lesson plan.

"You see?" he says, in the plural form addressing Ljubica, who is clinging desperately to the sleeves of his windbreaker. "Here three states meet in a common language. In peace, without arguments... We're going to celebrate half a century without war, do you understand?"

He looks around at the cluster of schoolchildren; they are still preoccupied with their squabbles. Many of them have already experienced the exploding rockets of war, and will again; replica rockets make no impression on them. Only Ljubica, sidestepping jabs to her ribs, nods in understanding. Which encourages the teacher to improvise: "Which one of you can name these three countries, these three non-warring neighbors?"

He gazes at the three flags with inspiration in his eyes, but no one volunteers. Only Ljubica brags: "There were three flags at Grandpa's, too, I used to go there on vacation." She raises her fingers and counts: "Serbian, one, Croatian, that's two, and... Bosnian." She sighs: "I don't go there anymore."

Consider yourself lucky, the teacher thinks to himself, uneducator-like. He loudly repeats his question: "So what are the names of the three states on the Rhine? Ljubica?" he urges her. The little girl drops her eyes and mumbles: "I need to pee, Mr. Pracák. Where?" The educator, dumbstruck, shrugs his shoulders. From the crowd of pupils someone hisses, not so loud as to give themselves away, but loud enough to be heard: "Go take a leak in the water, you Chetnik."

You can't step twice into the same classroom, the teacher Jan surmises, and not just since the painful discovery of his own fear in the face of his pupils. On board the floating restaurant, anchored squarely on the border of three states, he fears for his life publicly. Truth be told, however, he is now staring not into the taunting eyes of one of his lanky ten-year-olds, but into the unsmiling snout of a gun, the likes of which he himself, having opted for civil service instead of the military, has never held in his hands. One of the bantam Balkan brawlers, armed sufficiently by nature alone in the opinion of the none-too-tall pacifist Pražák, is leveling it at his teacher's chest.

The assailed vaguely recollects the practical advice of the police psychologist, which has since become a permanent point on the teachers' conference agenda: "Look your attacker straight in the eye," the psychologist repeats, "demand the weapon firmly and calmly. Wait, but do not repeat your demand. If appropriate, give a guarantee of no punishment. But try not to say too much. And above all, don't make a move!"

Out of all these instructions, the paralyzed Jan finds he is able to act only according to the last. Luckily the pistol-packing student merely shouts: "Bang!" like one of those cheery little bubbles in a comic strip. (Even so, the one at gunpoint is relieved. Just then it occurs to him, in a connected if abstract way, that the bark of gunfire is international, while the verbal transcription of the barking sounds changes with each language. In fact he doesn't know what it would sound like in his father's tongue, though he still remembers the stories his father used to tell in which the dogs barked ruff-ruff, unlike the mutts of his mother and the locals, whose yelping goes bow-wow.)

And the barking stops. The Serbian cub scout Milan volunteers his weapon to the teacher, commenting scornfully: "It's a fake. Just sounds like a real one. I took it from the Ustashas. They were scaring Ljubica with it."

He speaks about his Croatian classmates in the terminology of war, which does not belong here but cannot be driven away. It is omnipresent, in each and every one of us, adults and children alike. Everywhere that fear and hate have access. Thus reflects the teacher who has been assigned the impossible task: to cleanse from these children's souls the image of the world that surrounds them.

For it is not just in the Balkans that homes are burning. They are also burning in the heart of Europe. For probably the first time since the fiery sacrifice of Master Jan Hus, a pilgrim with a letter of safe conduct to protect him, both sides of the Rhine have ignited with hatred for newcomers – refugee shelters, dormitories for foreign workers, housing for foreigners. And in the yard of the Swiss school, in the homeland of Pestalozzi the educator and humanist, whose spirit and name come to life in the international villages of the children, died a small immigrant, attacked by his native classmates. Until then, the burning homes had claimed lives only occasionally, and the autopsy showed that the schoolboy had a weak heart. So the intention, it seems, is not to kill but to intimidate, to emphasize the right and the might of the native majority.

In revenge, though, minorities are arming themselves, and the violence, paradoxically pilloried by the media in sensationalist style, despite the dreadfulness of the topic, is spreading faster than the incendiary marches of xenophobes. Not just in the backwaters, but also in schoolyards, in train stations, in parks, just about everywhere in public, and even in private, it is not simply citizens fearing criminals, but the minority fearing the majority, the old fearing the young, the little fearing the big, the weak fearing the strong.

And this is precisely why tolerance has been placed in lesson plans as a topic involving more than just an explanation of individuals and nations living together in peace. But how does one teach tolerance in a world without love? Surely children are not the bewildered pilgrims whom Comenius advises in "Labyrinth of the World and Paradise of the Heart," his image of a violent world and merciful faith: "Return from whence you came, to the home of thy heart, and close the door behind you"? Children who have yet to leave their fathers' homes, but have already lost their homelands? Fugitives from the violence and war that are so unexpectedly gaining ground right here, on a border of peace?

Here is Milan, now doing battle with the allied Croatian-Albanian troopers blocking Ljubica's access to the ship washroom. By his side for some mysterious reason stand the Sicilians – ah yes, of course, the disinherited Antonio has locked himself into a toilet stall and is spitting out the window on his tormentors. Meanwhile the Kurds, in league with the Greeks, have hemmed in several of the Turks and are slowly edging them toward the bow of the ship, adorned with the flags of the neighboring states, but unprotected by any railing...

The teacher to no avail claps his hands and calls out unheard in an effort to prevent the worst. He casts himself into the fray, but without support feels overwhelmed. The logic of the ludicrous, perhaps now swelling into tragedy, causes him to slip on the watery deck and fall between the damp flagpoles, which he cannot catch hold of. He brakes in vain, even on the very tip of the deck, whose edging has been removed, probably for the sake of flag-raising ceremonies.

And in the midst of danger, Jan, like many a pacifist, reaches for his weapon. He frees his hand from the crush, pulls the confiscated bogus gun from out of his windbreaker, unlatches what his fingers decipher as the safety, and raises his hand with the pistol in it over the heads of the human tangle... Then aims somewhere into international waters and squeezes the trigger.

The river police patrol boat investigating the shooting on the border chugged away. Jan got off without a citation for disturbing the peace, and was even allowed to keep the pistol after they looked it over. Just in case he ever had trouble again capturing the attention of his pupils, the police recommended that he use a whistle.

The tolerance lesson, too, had long since lapsed, and in fact the police's explanation of the rules of the river, complete with demonstrations of boat maneuvers and flag signalling – so captivating the students that Antonio could leave the toilet in safety, freeing it up for Ljubica's use – swallowed up even the history lesson that was to follow. Still, the teacher reckons, the two complement each other, and the class, hard to believe but true, haven't let out a peep.

Now, of course, they have gone back to their noisemaking, and besides, class is over for the day. The teacher tentatively claps his hands and points out the stairs leading back to land. Which causes the pupils to disembark almost like first-graders, without a single objection or shout. Only two small figures fail to obey.

The teacher can't believe his eyes: Carmen and Mercedes, the twin models of discipline.

"Coming or not?" bellows the educator, his confidence now noticeably greater.

"I can't," whimpers one of the Swiss girls, hiding behind the border pillar under the French *tricouleur*.

"But the border is open here," says the puzzled teacher.

"She can't," explains her sister in tears from the Swiss side, "when she was in France she stepped in some..."

Rain breaks through the haze of Indian summer.

JAROSLAV VEJVODA (1940)
Essayist and novelist
Zürich

Miloš Vacík

TO A BABYLONIAN...

Babylonian, No, do not forsake
    your city
Its blackened anise and jasmine
    and bride's veil
Sycamore orchard in agony
    myrtle grove

From opulence of pride
    only ash under heel
Graves all around like burnt grass-tufts
And you go in fear among the ruins
    in which you rake seeking
the bone of God's hand And you find
    only your bone

I shall stay with you, whoever you are
For even with my last guttering breath
    I still believe
And I believe that you will believe

We will discourse together
    Each in his own language
And the word will not be a dagger It will be a word
For our respective gods we will hide
    in ourselves our rotunda
        our little cellar
For you there will be bread and salt
        and also wine
In the contentious days and nights
    of evil heavenly omens
we shall remain people for each other No I shall not

drive you and your children from your mahala
    from the house of your mother
You will not eat in the dark and in the darkness talk
In the dark make your bed and with carrion crows above
                              your head
    lie in the darkness
I shall not spray your house with fire
    And I shall not loose
into the November field of Alipash
among the school benches the bird of prey
    with a thousand splinters instead of feathers
to make the blood of seven dead cherubs
    flow under the door
I shall not kill your little sister Mirela
For your children I shall crack nuts
    And not their heads against the wall
I shall love them as my very self
Each in his own fashion we shall knead dough
    for our bread
I shall become you And you
    will become me
And neither my country nor yours
will be booty for your brothers or your enemies
Only this kneading-trough of earth will remain to us
    that will gather together our bones

Close. And ever closer to each other we lie
in the lucerne grass
    The sky above
strikes sparks While the tower falls
with the slightest creaking
    of the axis of the universe

Forty wars rage here in this world
The forty-first on Gallows Hill
like a colossal noose swinging in the wind
    Who will be caught out?

Do not let the head
of your aging gray mother grow cold
    Son of Earth
in the rustling of the raven stars

Babylonian, No, do not forsake
    your city

(An Excerpt)

MILOŠ VACÍK (1920)
Poet
Prague

Eva Kantůrková
DOUBTS ABOUT TOLERATION

The theme given to the 61st World Congress of International P.E.N. is "Literature and Tolerance." It is a key theme and I can deduce that the relationship between the two concepts – literature and tolerance – is meant positively. Indeed the theme seems to indicate that – if I want to appear cultured and noble-minded – I am intended to assume that tolerance benefits literature and that literature in particular cultivates tolerance; and that a writer, a member of the society of the noble-minded, is by profession a bearer of the spirit that is just what the times need. This quiet pressure enthralled me so much that I longed to try the theme out.

It is a wide theme, opening up many problems and subsidiary themes, and misgivings occur to me at every level. I will start with the first, that which creates the concept of literature, a literary work. As I call to mind the character of the great works just of my own national literature, a provocative question forces itself upon me: is tolerance relative to a literary work? The natural foundation, the strength through which a literary work originates is creativity, sometimes genius. But creativity is, from its deepest instinct, intolerant: it is based on creative originality. I would even go so far as to say that the intolerance of the poetics of a literary work, the intolerance of its spiritual and aesthetic uniqueness, is the direct source of the vitality of literature as an art form. Every newly discovered style of poetics mercilessly buries the previous one, is bitterly inimical to it; the one denies the other, one lives from the death of the other. It is a stuggle to decide the better. The only works that are tolerant are those that are eclectic, derivative, semi-inventive, conformist. Then literature endures as a kind of consumer good; it does not bother the reader with exclusive insurgency but simply, in its mediocrity, makes him or her feel like a consumer of literary quality, and allows its authors to rest comfortably in the embrace of gentle waves, in which a great leap is reduced to pulp and gradually flows into the net of literary boredom. But that billowing and whimpering cannot prevent a new leap, a new ninth wave, which breaks into the shallows and intolerantly sweeps them away. Which of us, wavering in our work between doubts and the will to overcome them, has not experienced this blow?

And I continue in opposition. Placing the concept of tolerance in relation to literature can also assign the task of examining which environments are harmful to literature and which are life-giving, how literature is treated in various environments and how it behaves in them. The environment of censorship is highly intolerant. The writer in Bohemia has in his or her genes the experience of books being burned, of their being banned and removed from libraries, schools and homes, and also of the imprisonment, interrogation, condemnation and even execution of undesirable authors. This list of splendid names starts in the Middle Ages with Jan Hus and could end in very recent times with Jan Zahradníček. Strangely enough, though, terrorism of the Middle Ages and modern times did not lead to the destruction of literature; on the contrary, through the effect of historical paradox, literature sooner or later turned into an urgent and positive impulse. Alphabetically last on the list, Jan Zahradníček, without pencil or paper, committed his poems to memory in prison, and his "The Sign of Power" is one of the miracles of Czech poetry. Among the grateful public a nimbus has grown around writers as a guild, the subjection of a literary work has become a symbolic act and the writer has become an esteemed prophet of freedom. In the mind of the public, writers fulfilled what the nation did not dare and did not even have the means to fulfill, because at the time when the modern likeness of the Czech nation was being formed, the Czechs had almost no power support and felt that the writer's word was their strongest shield. Yet as I describe this triumph of literature over intolerance, I realize with growing dissatisfaction that these meditations concern only outward circumstances. The inner dynamics of literary development – as I recall the works of authors on the same list – could not be confused either by persecution or by admiration, and literature became transformed and crumbled according to its own needs, regardless of these outward circumstances. The clash of ideas and poetics, passionate and intolerant, went on regardless of the gloom of censorship.

An offshoot of an intolerant environment, which may apply even in times of sovereign freedom, is under-education. One-way, one-dimensional (and I don't want to say straight out, ideological), self-complacent literary criticism, gazing into the shallows of personal taste, also seems to harm literature. But can even the most impertinent critic, in his predestined attitude to a work, add anything to it or take anything away? He can confuse the reader's opinion and taste, but that again is only an outward circumstance, separable from the work. And, in contrast to the period of censorship, the present-day stupid critic even has a certain asset: his criticism cannot lead to the author's arrest, nor can it become incriminating evidence before a totalitarian court. It is evidence only against himself, which seems to me quite just. So to close this passage of rebellious thoughts: as long as the external intolerant environment does not kill the author outright and the book is not burned, the environment remains without any basic influence on the author's writing. Or rather on the contrary, thanks to the effect of historical paradox, it strengthens the influence of the writing, so far, of course, as the author does not submit to self-censorship. However, that has nothing to do with tolerance, but again only with conformity, with those comfortable shallows of the author's livelihood.

And a third problem arises: whether the writer contributes in his or her work towards creating a tolerant environment. The idea of tolerance, in its opposition to totalitarian systems, to the misuse of the planet and nature by human rapaciousness, and to religious and ideological fundamentalists destroying human co-existence, has arisen as a life preserver. Civilization is searching for its spiritual paradise, the abracadabra to cure its difficulties, and supposes it will find it in self-restraint and a spirit of humility before the creator and creation. Tolerance really does smooth human relations and cultivate public activity; it is a civilizing value, similar, for instance, to respect for the dead. Public opinion considers being tolerant as an extraordinary feat belonging to those who are responsible for the culture of the social climate and milieu. For writers it is considered a duty. As I have already explained, it is extremely problematic in the literary sense. And in the social sense?

Writers usually perceive the dramas of their time very sensitively, but can they remain tolerant in them? I remember very well how we, who resisted intolerance, when driven into a corner by totalitarian pressure, practiced tolerance. But of whom were we tolerant? Of each other, though of different opinions, as we pressed into that corner against the wall; yet as soon as an opportunity came we willingly swept the regime away. And again various names occur to me. Emile Zola. Alexander Solzhenitsyn. Franz Werfel. Nikos Kazantzakis. Günter Grass. Tadeusz Konwicki. And can I, even in my work, be tolerant of the drama on the territory of Bosnia? When men there have not honor enough, in the first place, to protect their women and children from danger, and leave them at the mercy of what they themselves do to the women and children of those whom they call their enemies, who were yesterday their neighbors, I can only be paralyzed in horror and disgust at the madness of it – and search within myself for something more fundamental than just to be tolerant. Rather, solidarity with those who are suffering and against those who cause the suffering.

And in the anxiety of search, as one of our most sensitive seismographs of the times, the writer Dominik Tatarka, called his short story, I advance to the next theme. My reflections have so far moved in the extent and at the level of a single civilization, a single culture – Judeo-Hellenistic-Christian, if I want to convey its contents, and European-American, if I want to convey its geographical extent. But what about tolerance if the literatures of different civilizations meet? Do they pass one another by? Do they influence one another? Draw on one another? Do they deny one another? Or overlap? And can the idea of tolerance be used here at all, and how? In relationship to the culture of those worlds other than mine, the word tolerance seems to me to be almost insulting, full of missionary conceit.

Wherever I turn, the idea of tolerance appears to me to be inappropriate. But the wisdom of a word is greater than the lightness of human treatment of it, and so I will let my inadequacy be detected by the word. With what else but a word would a writer test him or herself? At the same time I apologize to the translator for the difficulty I am about to cause. The Czech word for tolerance, *snášenlivost,* is derived from the word *nést* – to bear. This word underwent a transformation in the depths of the ages. Originally the word *brát* – to take – had the meaning of the word *nést,* and *brát* was derived from the old Indian *bharami* – I bear. In a narrower sense it also meant to bear or carry a burden, fruit, a foetus, or directly to give birth, as has been preserved in English: *to bear* in Czech means all of to bear, to carry, to give birth and suffer and hold and support. And in German there is the word *ge-bären, geboren,* to bear fruit, to give birth. Is that not a wonderful solution? I carry, I tolerate or forbear, I take upon myself a burden, including something that is not my own, and my *snášenlivost,* my toleration, my taking, bears fruit.

Rebelliousness, what else, whispers to me, though, that a foetus originates from the clash of two elements, two cultures, two sexes, not from mutual tolerance; that it is a deeper and more penetrative act than tolerance can reach. But then, I oppose myself, if to bear, tolerate, respect, suffer, acknowledge, honor, or however else the idea of tolerance can be expressed, also means to take, bear a burden, give birth to, be enriched, and even to give the possibility of taking. I can only support the original given theme. Yes, there are deep relationships between literature and tolerance, two concepts of culture.

EVA KANTŮRKOVÁ (1930)
Novelist
Prague

Pavel
Šrut

THE PLAINT
OF HOMER'S WIFE

What with a man who waits for the ebb
to set off in the wake of Odysseus?
What with the woman to whom returns only the high tide?
(When I drift into sleep I am an aviary
and within it the imprisoned birds bear me)

No, I don't complain
I don't say only yesterday...
And I'm not going blind with tears
like this man of mine
when he loses his sight over the verses
and has only a table in place of sails

Oh, don't believe it
He never set sail

Pavel
Šrut
GALILEO'S
WIFE

For love alone she would rather do a dirty deed
rather rat on the telescope

Not Galileo!

Alone she knocks together an affidavit and apprehensively
affixes
the treacherous incriminating evidence

It trysted regularly with Luna
this field glass this phallus
that pokes the heavens...

Not Galileo!

Which she would sign, even before the council,
with her own monthly blood

Pavel
Šrut

THE LANDLADY
WONDERS
ABOUT STUDIOSO
FAUSTA

Incognito if necessary
this one of mine is usually curly-haired
and I always arise a mite early
to lay on his threshhold in time
a mug of scorched black
unsweetened ersatz coffee
And I wonder
how so much soot gets in the house
and I wonder why always only in the dark
and why we may not
be like God created us, naked
And I wonder why he
inserts the parchment into me beforehand like a membrane
and solemnly swears never to leave
through the door like the others
and I wonder
if the pain
I feel during all this
is not from the draft –

PAVEL ŠRUT (1940)
Poet, lyricist, translator
Prague

Jan
Trefulka
THE NEVER-ENDING
MINUTE

The older he got, the more urgently he realized that with each awakening to a new day he must be born again, that within a few split seconds – the period increased with growing age, eventually, perhaps, it would be many minutes – he must once again search for and find his time, his history, his relationships, his identity. For sleep increasingly resembled death; more and more often he spoke with the dead in his sleep, and yet, and still, the border between dreaming and waking, even in daylight, tended to be vague and unsteady. There were times when it was difficult for him to distinguish between what he had actually experienced and what he had dreamed, what he was doing and what he was merely calling up from memory; there were even times when he was surprised to have a third person confirm the reality of his experiences.

He knew that all these were signals of the end now more or less distant, but death announcing itself in this way seemed to him an event free of all horror, in fact, free of any importance whatsoever, a mere non-arousal from sleep, an inability to return from a dream. He theorized that if everyone were guaranteed such a truly humane way of perishing, it would be worth more than a hundred per cent guarantee of life, safeguarded from all possible forms of suffering. He theorized that the human organism should have been equipped with a universal sensor which, by analyzing the workings of vital processes in the body and the mind, could reliably and automatically determine the optimum moment of non-arousal, without any forebodings or anxieties; a sensor capable of taking into account not only chemistry, pressure and stress, but also one's pain threshold and will to live, and capable of establishing a degree of suffering that is still tolerable and does not exceed the point at which the person-

ality breaks down and shrivels up, transforming the human being into nothing but a temple to the fear of death.

He wasn't able to shake his memories of the long year of dying
he had spent with his father, the gradual departure of his senses
and wits. His eyes had been the first to betray him: the old man
began to complain of tiny letters and poor-quality print; he
started reading with the help of a magnifying glass, an ordinary
one at first, a watchmaker's later; but even enlarged, the letters
broke down and warped to the point of illegibility. His Dad's
world was a shambles, all at once his handwriting swerved out
of line, and his brain was suddenly no longer capable of guiding
his hands to perform the craftsman's work and repairs around
the house that had once occupied him.

The uncommon stillness of his father's brain cells brought on
depressions and feelings of emptiness; before long, hallucina-
tions filled up the emptiness, as if his deformed vision were elic-
iting faulty connections. His mind, deliberating logically up until then, began to fantasize, wrenching words out of context and
fabricating for them nonexistent associations; no sooner were
syllables overheard or seen than they changed into words unut-
tered and unread. The piecemeal messages of his feeble senses
were supplemented to the point of absurd wholeness.

First he started to see children in his bedroom, lounging
around on chairs and disappearing the second he approached
them. He was calm and rational when he talked about them,
these mirages constructed by his age-impaired vision; but as
time went on, they grew from his emptiness and anxiety into the
shadows of men who he believed were threatening him, bur-
glars, violent attackers, even agents of the secret police. When
that happened, his father would call him and he would have to
go downstairs to the big bedroom. There was a time when his
father could be calmed with words and an explanation; eventually, though, his flights of fantasy became more persuasive and
more powerful than any arguments reason could offer.

The old man was convinced that even his son had forsaken
him; he ate less and less and wouldn't take his pills; when his
son insisted, he pretended that he couldn't swallow them.
He couldn't even run away from his visions anymore, because

his legs weren't strong enough to carry him, and when they found him one morning lying on the floor chilled to the bone, it was clear that the only solution left was to put him in the hospital.

He would have been happy to let his dad die at home in bed; as a result, compounding his morning ritual of self-searching, from then on, was a feeling of shame at his weakness. At the time he just hadn't been able to bring himself to provide that most intimate of care for the immobile and estranged body of a person whose soul, too, had now become estranged – not so estranged, however, that he didn't have the presence left to rouse himself to a mistaken and yet somehow plausible understanding of the situation when the ambulance drivers were loading him onto the stretcher. Just then he remembered his son explaining to him the previous day that they were going to take him away to the hospital, and suddenly he ceased to believe that they were taking him to the pulmonary ward with pneumonia and thought they were sending him away to the local insane asylum for psychiatric care. He fought with all the physical strength he had left, and after a long fight he said out loud with conviction and composure: "I never would have thought, Pavel, that you could be so cruel."

That was the last sentence his father bequeathed him. Once he arrived at the hospital he stopped recognizing anyone. In the hours leading up to his death he had counted on and on, reciting endless strings of numbers – as if all that were left of him was an amazing mechanism which someone had enabled to multiply multi-figure digits from memory.

And the knowledge that the sentence had been unjust, that his own conscience was clean by any human standards, didn't help. For nearly an entire decade his ninety-one-year-old father had lived with them after the death of his mother, and they had cared for him conscientiously, even at the expense of reduced or cancelled vacations; they had never exchanged sharp words with him, he had never been in the hospital before, no one had ever thought about putting him into a retirement home. But still the son felt guilty, if only because those words, however untrue, could even be uttered.

And so each and every day, as he was being born into the next hours of life, before anything else, he had to come to terms with the painful, sad and humiliating newsreel of his faults. One memory led to another, they came individually, in pairs, in whole gaggles; not just in two-dimensional black-and-white, but in color, with shapes, saturated with smells, sickly and sweet alike, words, thumps. He would fight his way slowly through them to full consciousness: it's me, with my fate; it's morning and I'm alive and once again I have to perform the motions and do the work that has been meted out to me, even though I don't know why and most of what I do is not even interesting for me anymore, let alone enjoyable.

He saw the curtain that separated the double bed from the rest of the living room – his only room, albeit a large one, acting as both kitchen and study. Due to his unfortunate habit of searching for meaning in everything he came across, he began searching for the designer's idea in the curtain pattern: a girl on a horse, holding a parasol or an umbrella over her head, and the falling figure of a boy, reaching out his hand in vain for a ball, and all of this floating as if in weightless space. It was neither ugly nor kitschy, but what annoyed him was its fundamental lack of logic – to stylize a circus show, if not a story, into the role of an ornament, one hundred falling boys and balls, one hundred girls dancing on horseback – it felt like blasphemy to him, the degradation of a scene of poetry and the actors in it. He realized, of course, that he was overreacting and could just as well have taken the endless repetition as a whimsical game or a symbol of the repeating realities of human life. Frivolity, however, was not in his nature, he had not been blessed with the ability to perceive the beauty of collectivity, with the fascination of throng performance, and for him the images of the Spartakiáda group gymnastics were a degradation of humanity, an expression of the mindless acceptance of the way things were.

Following the light, his eyes found not a window, but a low, broad vent along the ceiling of the dreary space, like a cubbyhole in the corner of a warehouse behind a store on the edge of town that a shopkeeper's apprentice would live in. There was a shelf of clumsy construction, holding boxes, bottles and glass jars for preserves filled with spices, little sacks and vessels, parts of kitchen appliances and pieces of dishes from services shattered long ago. Mesh sacks of potatoes, lemons and onions lay about on the floor in the corner, and the blend of odors that every so often wafted his way through the penetrating cold morning air also carried the smell of garlic and leeks.

But next to his bed stood a wardrobe, and nailed to the top of it was a small set of shelves made of old planks that reached all the way up to the ceiling – three tiers of books on it, and only the lowest and most accessible tier occupied by two-pound packages of sugar, flour and salt, and, in smaller packages, lentils, beans and rolled oats.

Had it not been for the round illuminating object on the opposite wall, it could have been a still life from the shop of a Czech patriot in a little village at the foot of the Krkonoše Mountains in the middle of the last century. Did this curious juxtaposition of Hemingway, Lenin, semolina and matrimonial bed express the burdensome demands of life? A lifestyle? Or was it a liberal disregard for the conventional order of a bourgeois dwelling?

No doubt a little of everything, for not a single thought or feeling, not a single fateful event ever fully matured within him. Decade after decade he had considered this a personal shortcoming; he had admired the brilliance and consistency of confident artists and thinkers, their perfectly logical conceptions and lines. It was only with increasing age and experience that he realized that ambiguousness, incompleteness and imperfection were the infallible signs of human normality, and that those people who mercilessly pursue and carry out their logically faultless, brilliant and irrefutable ideas are either lunatics or criminals.

For any intelligence, any knowledge, learning or behavior that seeks only a rational justification for the realization of projects – at their core always precarious on account of their inhuman one-sidedness – exterminates man more surely and thoroughly than all the ridiculous but invariably short-winded bursts of passion put together.

With time he found an excuse for the wanderings of his youth – after all, it had always been that way. Countless reconstructions and extensions had arisen on the foundations of crumbling cathedrals. At one time people had poured enormous sums of money into them without ever actually being able to explain what made a Gothic church any more useful and beautiful than a Romanesque one, or why both of those had to be torn down and reshaped into Baroque style, only so that centuries later in the next street over someone could erect a building that looked like a copy of a Greek temple.

Oh no, genius is not the crazed explorer of the outermost imaginable extreme, the fanatic of crystal clarity, of brilliant logic and faithfulness to principle; genius is the awareness of one's imperfection, by the realization that man and the world are so multifaceted that any law, any truth, any scientific evidence can, under the right circumstances, be violated, refuted, transformed into its opposite; that man has already been all that exists in the universe – ray, gas and stone – and there is no reason why a trace of all that should not be left behind in his mind, just as the fish and the flying lizard have remained in his fundamental cellular material, along with the murders through which he has sustained and defended himself and his awareness of community, born of the experience that humans are incapable of living alone.

Yet it was to solitude that he woke, day in and day out, although not because he didn't have a wife, children and friends. The solitude was not within him; it emanated from the world that surrounded him. The societal system – swearing from its inception by solidarity, collectivity and socialism, words whose original meaning conveyed selflessness, solace, mutual understanding and charitable work on behalf of a life that was to be meaningfully ordered, agreeable and open to human friendship – had at one point seemed to him to be hypothetically worthwhile, reasonable and possible, despite that in practice it devoured and destroyed lives (even that he could explain away); that system, as a result of incompetent policies locally and ignominious doctrines abroad, had changed his country into one enormous apartment complex of embittered and solitary people.

Each morning as he woke with difficulty, he was visited by every type of solitude his country had been exuding for the last

twenty years. Again and again he was forced to realize with
deep-seated anxiety what it was he was waking up to and how
many years had gone by since the last time he had woken up to
a clear and sunny morning that had been a clear and sunny
morning for him too. Now he would regard a day like that as a
moment of unspeakable happiness. For what else could happiness mean except no insurmountable barrier of lies and unde-
fined interdictions standing between people and the world surrounding them – whenever he wanted to reach out and touch the
space he moved in; whenever he wanted to call out and greet the
people he wanted to greet. What else but that a clear and sunny
day would not present an unwitting counterpoint to the atmosphere of the environment he had to step into, with the dreary
dusk in which he had to live.

The hardest waking of all was when he saw the sun shining
outside the window and heard the swifts crying out in the blue
sky high above. Surely it would take so little, he told himself:
just stop thinking about the filth, just stop thinking about the
past, the beauty, the honor, the love, and be grateful that the sun
was shining even on that orphaned and pilfered strip of land.
Surely it would take so little, just a crumb of human understanding, a pebble of courage, a whiff of a truthful word.

Except that the truthful word is a myth, like the philosophers'
stone or the elixir of life. Ever since he had begun writing, all he
could think of was expressing the idea that concentrated in each
moment, in each decision, each look, gesture and sound is every
little thing a person has experienced, whether consciously or
subconsciously, alone or by his or her ancestors, as a human and
as an animal, as a stone, as gas, as a mortal being and as a witness, not as a participant in that unimaginable instant in which
the universe was conceived.

A genius does not invent; genius is the ability to recall the ice
cold of the universe and the furnace blast of suns, the pressures
within the folding rocks and minerals, the instincts of the dino-
saurs and the rustling of grasses over mouse trails trampled
smooth. To experience the birth and death of one's ancestors, to
die with the dread of the murdered and tremble with the bliss of
the simple souls who believed in miracles. And for that, for all

that, a person has nothing but a mathematical equation, his or her own body, his or her brain, tone, color, soil, stone, words.

He was overcome with vertigo to think that contained in every second of human decision-making were the experiences of every one of person's ancestors and hundreds of millions of years of gradual transformations of matter. It would take thousands of pages of handwriting to express precisely in words one single instant in the life of one single human, and even then, it could never be complete. A reader could spend his or her whole life reading through the account of an act that lasted a single minute and still never reach the end. And yet it is precisely this inherent inability of an individual work of art to express the motives of human behavior in their entirety that ensures art eternal life.

JAN TREFULKA (1922)
Novelist
Brno

Miroslav Huptych
THE RED,
THAT IS,
ROYAL KITE

The nest of the kite is always found in the highest branches of trees,
especially the magnificent magnolias and white oaks.

A. E. BREHM, ANIMAL LIFE

We won't allow on the journey those who have domestic temperaments,
those who are fat, or those used to having everything. We will select only
those who still live in the manner of couriers, or the kind who travel
often on ships to India and are used to living only on biscuits, garlic,
frozen fish, in general fare that is far from palatable. The most suitable
for such a journey are shrivelled old women who have possessed since
childhood exceptional cleverness, and who know how to ride the backs
of goats by night, on pitchforks or on shabby old coats – and to fly on
them through huge aerial spaces.

JAN KEPLER, THE DREAM OF LUNAR ASTRONOMY

I'm calling you on a trip to Lunania
Arise somnambulist arise!
Your coat made of leaves and rain is ready
The staircase is the jaws of the house
but that is not your path
it's for bags full of grub
You must take the window Come somnambulist
I call you on a trip to Lunania
tonight will disembowel your life
It's going to turn you upside down
This demonic poker's going to penetrate you
any spiritual stuffing will lose its value
let your eyelids fall and come
All the chairs in the house are clawing with impatience
like horses whose water was laced with uppers
Tonight is going to dilate your pupils

which will devour the moon-god
followed by fish and howling dogs
It's going to be a night of busted antennas
a night to strip the wings off junebugs
a night to put bats' eyes on your plate
a night of lascivious maidens floating on their hair
into shameful pleasure
this'll be the night the frozen souls come creeping out
of cellars
where they vegetated with potatoes
it'll be a night when blazing hummingbirds
fly into the faces of pedestrians
a night when Tanit the Phoenician goddess of the moon
climbs onto the roof of your house
where will reach the stench of the holocaust
of first-born children
The cruel goddess Tanit will raise herself up amongst the
hissing snakes
like a rose in the undulating grass
you will hear: Come somnambulist
you with your plum-like eyes you with the blackberry eyes
pull yourself out of that muck of despair
tear apart your pillow and a swarm of flies will vanish
come I have a sacrificial knife obsidian blacker
than any imaginable darkness
will penetrate your chest
will extirpate all filth
the dung of your debased ideals
you will become light the wind will whistle across your bones
it'll be a song that will mock the blows of life
that make a mess of your head
it'll be a song that does not recognize the good spreading
like a pancake on the forehead of the prison warden
it'll be a song that with imaginary needles
will stitch the democratic web of the sky
within the horizon of a cloud of birds
who bring snow-white cloths not only to the vases of the night
but especially with them cover their hands

into which droops the heavy head of the melancholic
toying with suicide like a domesticated rat
It'll be a song which Tanit dances among the snakes
It'll be a song about an open window
it'll be a bewitching song: Come somnambulist come!
I call you on a trip to Lunania
Let your eyelids fall
and come – – –
You will awaken on a bed of lilies
David will play on his harp
and you will finally understand:
        The key to the stable with the Tragedy
        you do not clench in your pocket
        The Tragedy nonchalantly devours even the actors
        who look it straight in the eyes
        The Tragedy has the deep, endless eyes
        of stupid cattle
        and looks at you
        like a goose into a bottle
        and sees that there is neither wine nor truth
        only the hangover of the drowned
The drowned swim in my head
according to the theory of Aristotle
that the brain is the wettest part of the body
At the moment I have a flood in my brain There is a herd
of antelopes at a phosphorescent sea waiting for
the sea to write a poem about a kite
until the sea declares the Moon the vitamin C of poetry
and scurvy a national disease
The sea writes for every antelope an unusual toothless poem
and each one has a different half-life for disintegration
some disintegrate immediately after reading
While I'm trying to marry off the antelopes for wind
they transform into a herd of ideas
with the form and content of a piglet

Arise somnambulist arise!
I'm calling you on a trip to Lunania

Once again I'm going to smoke until morning like
a crematorium
If I were a dog
I would howl
(in the Mexican temples they used to sacrifice dogs
to the god of the moon)

Once again I find myself the morning after
at the window
oh how beautiful you are Moon!
how tenderly you extinguish the heavens
whose internal secretions give birth to the morning mists
preparing to engender puddles
which will be the womb
of earthworms and slugs

Oh how everything is connected by fibers of abstraction!

I catch myself again
sticking my fingers into the soil of the geraniums
At the sight of the first morning walkers
I finally comprehend
that each is searching for
his own path
to death

Under their nails
black half-moons

MIROSLAV HUPTYCH (1952)
Poet
Prague

Alexandr Kliment

NOTES ON THE GIVEN THEME

Literature and tolerance. An attractive pair, right from birth: bright, euphoric and restless twin girls. Only someone who truly loves them does not confuse their names. They are difficult to bring up and will be eternally young; one will not want to go to her deathbed as an old maid, and the other will bring lots of problem children into the world. I am watching them now in a decent commercial society and am amused to see what trouble they are going to make next. One of the girls upsets her tea and keeps on reciting verses. The other is silent, as if she were mute, which makes her parents and grandparents ashamed before the gallery of bankers, editors-in-chief, critics, politicians and post-modern loafers. But the second little girl had taken seriously to heart what they had hammered into her head: Don't interrupt when someone is speaking, silly-billy!

Bananas need no tolerance to grow. They are fertilized, ripen and rot; so it is and why should it be otherwise. But harvesting bananas, that is a whole set of problems! Transporting them, maintaining the proper temperature, selling, consuming and disposing of the skins ecologically, if they are not to serve the treacherous banana-skin effect, when the fool slips and bashes his head on the pavement. Mechanics also deal with tolerance very skillfully, for instance when fitting parts or in the contact of wheels and rails. Shopkeepers standing behind the scales count with tolerance a bit more than customers standing in front of the scales. Public opinion polls tolerate a certain percentage of nonsense. Royal punctuality is a constant concept only because it is the king himself who holds the stopwatch. Plus or minus a second or an hour or two is part of the charm of every date and of the boredom of waiting on the platform. If we do not achieve the

best, at least we avoid the worst and in practice we put a finger
on a tolerable average of however many intolerable coexistences
life brings. An average ceases to frighten us if it is statistically
confirmed. The average product per capita. The average weight
of a woman. The average age of a man. This civic and generally
cultivated virtue of mini-tolerance would not deserve contempt
if it did not spawn a policy of the art of the possible. We can
make no compromise with death. Tolerance has nothing to do
with compromise. Tolerance is the art of the impossible, the voluntary coexistence of love and hatred, a diplomatic recognition
of death within the perspective of life. But a writer exists to be
good at something, not to average global phenomena.

Tolerance would not arise without conflicts. Tolerance does not
occur anywhere outside human comedies and dramas. Without
conflicts there would be no literature. Tolerance is an invention
of humanism and therefore of respect for conflict. But decency
does not lie in the basis of either life or literature.

The galaxy does not know the difference between the little shop
on the corner and the supermarket. Atomic energy does not recognize the difference between the speed of a velocipede and that
of a car. Absolute movement is at the same time absolute stillness. In the universe both yes and no apply, without upsetting
the balance. Matter is changed into energy and vice versa, entirely without commitments. There is no tolerance in an atomic
nucleus, but if we start poking it about, to be better able to grill
kidneys or liver, we smash up the whole world.

We do not need to define what is black on white. What is written
is given, and we proudly call these neglected memorials to immortality literature. But they are letters. Picasso was once
asked to contribute a few drawings to the collection of the greatest painters of the century. He drew the alphabet. Nothing more.
He had drawn everything. But what tolerance is, is a question as

tricky as life itself. It is impossible at the altar to say yes and at
the same time no, yet the institution of marriage itself bears
testimony to the fact that tolerance can turn tragedy into come-
dy and that everyday life can recommend rather different worries than those of metabolism and energy exchange.

An author can be bribed by good intentions or bad money, but in
that moment he or she leaves the empire of freedom and fantasy
and enters the world of ideology and trade. In literature, as opposed to journalism, nothing is flexible. Journalism reacts
quickly. Literature slowly creates. Literature cannot be tolerant
if it is to remain virgin. And yet it is an example of tolerance. If
you want to – read! If you don't want to – don't read! You like it,
you don't like it. But if you vote for a crook or a tolerant politician, your children's lives are already dependent on it. A possible
expression: the critic tore the author to pieces. Yet the author
continues to write. It is worse if the critic is the state, which forces the judiciary to condemn the poet to exile or death. Violence
against poetry is as old as a song it has not yet known how to
write. There is no instrument of force against readers. On the
rack you close your eyes, and in the worst case you read A and
think B. Millions of unread books line the path of retreat by
dictatorships.

With some exaggeration I would connect literature with tolerance in the case of those authors whom the reader accuses of
amorality, unscrupulousness and indifference. They turn a
cheerful story into desperation and we don't know why. They
describe human scum with humor and make them so interesting
that they rival the angels. As long as tolerance is to have any
deeper meaning than the rules of democratic behavior, then it is
just the willingness to talk not only with the opposition, but
with the enemy, and the will to understand the incomprehensible. Only here does tolerance get rid of tactical and operational
functions and go to the root of the matter: I shall try to face up
to futility and a life without motive.

Just because the writer is so intolerant in his or her demands on the role of characters in an imaginary story, he or she considers it a duty to be committed in favor of tolerance in civic life. A completed story that can no longer be rewritten, differently and better, warns me against any kind of unambiguous solution in practice, against granting the human permanent citizenship and the inhuman permanent homelessness. Tolerance is seeking an alternative where there is none. And it is a good thing that this art is inspired by a novel whose quality the reader refuses on principle.

I adore spacious aristocratic parks and little cottage gardens. There intention and care for effect are married to the creativity of nature. But I must admit that even an overgrown forest and weeds have something to be said for them, and so far I have not had the honor of being landed straight in the jungle. I hope it is still rampant somewhere. Where is the border between literature and printed matter? Between journalism and propaganda? We all know this boundary, but we can't map out the terrain. It is as uncertain as the border between mental health and psychopathy, as between the performance of a conjurer and swindler. But let's not confuse uncertainty with tolerance. Let's not legitimize tolerance in order to find an alibi.

An author can be a very tolerant humanist. We can feel this attitude from his or her approach to the material, but the way it is worked up cannot be tolerant of anything. It is possible, though unprofitable, to make over a coat, but we can't reweave the material; it is such as it is. The author can discuss his or her story endlessly, but the story itself cannot at any price apologize to anyone even once. Wanting literature to be tolerant is a misunderstanding. But an intolerant author will never write anything interesting.

Tolerance is not an atmosphere, but individual behavior. I guarantee my text, but my text does not guarantee me. That is a professional risk that results from the fact that I address at least two readers at once, of whom one is certainly anonymous. My colleague von Goethe must reckon with the fact that after more than a hundred years someone may shoot himself for unrequited love, though, as proved, Goethe never recommended it to anyone. It will always be somehow on two rails. We will put a pistol into Werther's hands and act as best man at a friend's wedding. No tolerance, when it is a question of the point!

There are enviable examples of tolerance that we read in personal letters. But that's another story. These documents were not intended for publication, although their perfect stylization makes them seem as if the author knew that they would one day become an example of the closest links between literature and life, and they can expect the highest estimation of authenticity. Let us be tolerant even of sacrilege, especially when not even one of the participating sides protests against it at a confession mediated by the mail.

A joyless opinion, a lie established as a world order, was expressed in Prague not long ago by a certain Josef K. We shall not argue as to what percentage of truth there is in it, but it is certain that Franz Kafka described his state of helplessness well, and that this good description of bad things did not contribute to an improvement of morals, but the reverse. In the scenery of Sarajevo, philosophy, art and religion appear unnecessary. But we who want to believe in something, to say the least in our own words, will cultivate this trivial Cinderella even among ruins. I do not know if we really belong where we are, awakening from romantic dreams and rational heresies (that is to say, on the rubbish dump) but we are where we are. Thanatology takes on greater importance than obstetrics, and waste produces more problems than production itself. Shall we still be tolerant of ourselves?

In the world of science and trade the writer is a dilettante. And what is left? A museum on the rubbish dump. Though after all a writer can help something a little bit with a few human fighting words. But first he or she must achieve authority with, for instance, some cheap kitsch or respect for the incomprehensible. The incredible tolerance of the public.

In the first place we must get rid of the complex of intellectual sovereignty. Only then can we begin to help cultivate tolerance under such difficult conditions as the daily grind, obsessed by aversions and sympathies, weighed down by love and hatred, determined by policy and riddled with politicking. Cultivating tolerance does not mean supporting the function of the referee, who pushes two impassioned wrestlers apart in the ring according to the rules. Only when we see the situation as a whole and give selfish love an ecological dimension shall we be able to help something. To make every ideal of happiness relative and recommend coexistence with an active enemy are more purposeful than are worries about keeping alive an enemy who is defeated.

It is not at all true that money decides everything. As long as there is no shooting it is words that decide everything, including money; but their power has to be first agreed upon by at least two sides. That we all know how to sign our names would in itself lead to chaos, if we did not force grammar rules into that element. I don't mean rules like the highway code or spelling, but art... I am thinking of the art of tolerance, which I cannot define, but which I can compare to the art of the pause. Taking a little distance from things. A moment of stillness in the drama. A short silence in the conversation. The Germans know that well when they say that in a moment of silence an angel passes. Russians, before they start out on a journey, sit for a while in silence. What Czech pause do we have in the heart of Europe? The cry of the good soldier Švejk: "Don't shoot, there are people here!"

Kruschev, to whom we owe the first erosion of the Stalinist monolith, spoke an unforgettable sentence. He came to a village where the co-op members complained that the rain got into the cowshed, although they had passed several important resolutions on the matter. Nikita Sergeyevitch said, "Comrades, you won't roof the cowshed with resolutions or reports!" Our novels, as long as they are well written, report on our anxiety, perhaps even with a little humor, but they will not renew the ruins we live in.

ALEXANDR KLIMENT (1929)
Novelist
Prague

Jana
Štroblová
THE CLOSED
GATE OF GOLD

The view from the Mount of Olives, which he surveys through
                                    sunlight as if through sorrow:
cemeteries, camps without the stronghold,
beneath the banners
of various faiths
they storm – lo! – Jerusalem. When will open
the Gate of Gold, this healed-over wound in its side
which, closed and bricked up through the blazing sun and
                                         storm of
bony eternity, withstands the rap of a knuckle...? Does only
                                           God
have its golden key?
Now hear the march of the years, there go
                                     tombstone-footprints
of superhuman proportion, the footprints of decayed
pilgrims, toiling toward the stronghold, the hillside of the
                                       Holy City,
to the foot of the Gate of Gold, Oh Lord oh God,
and all for this reason: that
when the Last Judgment arrives
and your heavenly steeds and herald angels storm the gate,
all the camps of the dead will want to be the first to stand
                                   before your countenance!
The very countenance before which, while they still lived,
                                   until their deaths,
they felled the innocent sacrificial lamb
and splashed blood; before your own very eyes
they smashed the altars of others and roasted them on their
                                   own spits,
God, your pious ones! Godless they weren't, you know; they
                           honored you, they knew the fear of God,

sacred reverence gripped them,
in the stone they knelt out a hollow or kissed one out with
their mouths,
and so they glorified a temple, their own temple, which they
proclaimed as yours,
where they believed that you swore by their belief,
your voice, that they will draw into their speaking trumpets.
But they read in the voices from heaven
only their own wills to abusive power. They made themselves
prophets
so that each of them afterward
can be called by name as the first prophet
when the heavens are sundered and the earth disappears
beneath the feet
of your armies. Then – certainly swords too, not just
trumpets and brass.
And the Judgment Day
they wish to see as a war ("Whose faith throws its flames
the furthest?")
like that they carry out all their lives in the Holy City,
where the Wailing Wall complains vainly,
walled in by hate. Walls of hate, streets of hate
like streets of "love." Watchtowers
and church steeples. Bells with casings and without...
blessed items –
the market: Who will give more? ("Sold, one
consecrated picture!") Candles, holidays,
God's feasts and fasts, Ramadan, Easter, Shabbat, Sunday –
the Lord's day
and then sin again: the victim's blood ("The Lord has promised
you one hundred blows!")
and a clamor, a din,
emotions
(For the Bible! For the Koran! ... Let all that is vain perish in
God's name!)
The City of God's visitation.
And after visitation – forgiveness?
Whose God will pardon us?

Jana Štroblová

EXPULSION FROM PARADISE

Was it paradise or not? Even if we call into question the
tender friendship of the wolves and lambs, and the
green pastures
where the blue flax blossomed pinkly,
there remains the apple. The fruit with the blush,
colored by original sin. How innocently pure
nakedness was until then! Just two playful souls
paddling in the dew without even trampling the fresh grass.
Why was Eve dallying with the snake? Was Adam to blame?
Longing? She had a fancy for something, didn't know what.
A body?
There were no bodies yet. Providence was cloaked in
indistinctness,
and Adam's rib, adjacent to something resembling Eve's heart,
had until then been no more than a thought. A wing of light.
Nevertheless it was precisely this rib that caused her
to flutter
(this thing, familiar yet strange,
this ambiguity between calling voice and vision,
this waking lullaby – "la la"
for which she fell into a torpid longing...)
and now the punishment is due, even if just God's sword
flaming,
even if only a fig leaf! No, a fig leaf
is a pretext for metaphor – cheat and deceit,
the punishment is the body – flesh bones skin,
a costume change body. Soul sewn into a skin
and hurled to the world!
Here the man's rib gets stuck in the woman like an unfused
bone.

It's no longer just longing, this anger, that he – suddenly
                              stiff – sticks into her
(a hard kernel into marrow,
a straight line into curves of doubt,
roe and gills into fish,
a wing or a rib into a woman,
the knife of the Beginning already plunged into the living)
and the prelapsarian quiet is lost;
anger will lead her through bare existence. And when now
                              and then she lets herself go,
then love.

Jana Štroblová

THE ARK
OF TOLERANCE

Earlier, in the time of the Flood, there lived Noah,
old Noah, who led aboard his Ark
all that lived and breathed on Earth, pair after pair,
and spake not "This one yes – this no,
this has tasty meat, while the other
could suddenly eat one of my own, for instance"
and spake not "Only we, only I
decide which of these less powerful ones
will be no more." He let the Earth decide which should live,
but she had long since decided: she created them all without
difference,
man alongside the wolf, lion and mouse.
We, meanwhile, had taken pains to sort
the beasts from the people, the seed from the chaff,
so that everything mixed together at once
and nothing is left... a few tribes,
which we painstakingly lead across the wasteland –
our vassals, taken into grace so that they may preserve us,
so they may breathe for us with their mouths.
Except that Noah was not saving himself, but the Earth...

JANA ŠTROBLOVÁ (1936)
Poet and translator
Prague

Alexandra Berková
...LITERATURE AND TOLERANCE...

tolerance...
tolerance... brrr – disgusting word;
to tolerate: to abide, to carry, to bear; from the Latin *tolerare*,
tollere: to carry from the foundation; *tul* – *tuli* – I carried, "in
connection with a burden..." Yes, certainly: tolerance is indeed
a stance toward the foreign: What is tolerance, something
close to me?
1781 A.D.: Edict of Tolerance: freedom of belief in the Czech
lands for 167 years. Which came first, tolerance or intolerance? Is such an edict necessary in a tolerant land?
to tolerate: to abide, to put up with, to be forbearing: I turn it
over in the mouth like a caterpillar...
tolerable: bearable, relatively agreeable, something which can
be endured, something which can be suffered...
Who was the first to take upon himself this gigantic burden of
accepting that the world is diverse...?
... that someone else has a different god, different skin color, a
differently shaped skull, different desires?
... no two identical snowflakes have ever fallen upon the
earth's snout. Only the human spirit, free as a pendulum,
oscillates stiffly between Yes and No, and gives itself wrinkles
over whether to accept the world as it is...
... how much tolerance does the finch need to come to terms
with the existence of the sparrow?
... the stupid animal Man has raised fences of categories,
ramparts of universalities and walls of abstract judgments;
blocked windows with a wealth of words and in the name of
logic created foreigners from the remainder of the world...

tolerability: endurability, bearability, had it up to here: here
yes, but there no. The tolerance of this screw's 0.5 to 0.7
millimeters, ma'am, not a bit more. This, that is, this tolerance has got its limits, you understand. If it don't have its
limits, it ain't tolerance, ma'am, is that clear?

... and this stupid animal Man has turned everyone against
him and himself against everyone – and put himself up on a
pedestal to drive... only to find then that to get a view out of
the pit of ideas you need the ladder of tolerance: this man
wants a bit of the boy, to master himself and deal with the
existence of this strange, incomprehensible tangle of divergent
ideas, this inarticulate mass of some strange, peculiar, *other*
Not-I...

... and the stupid animal Man, cowering behind his walls,
envies the cat's freedom and creates an uproar in order to kill
the time that still remains, or whines in horrible loneliness
and calls his brothers in the vicinity:

calls with prose as well as verse and color and tone...

ALEXANDRA BERKOVÁ (1949)
Novelist
Prague

Zdeněk Rotrekl

SOMETIMES WHEN PEOPLE MEET

Sometimes when people meet
they're old with youth
and young with age
They come to each other across the blades of knives –
They give up their shadows to a cloak-room of memories
and words
(the attendant takes no payment for a coat
compassion won't allow her to
when the visitors are compassionate
– and they usually are –)
A moving being resurrects
forgotten words
Liquid warmth flows
from unseen springs

How close we are in our silence
– we leave our coats and umbrellas in the cloak room

Yet she knows what to do with them

Together we exit into coffins of unseen light
into coffins of exactly the same wood

ZDENĚK ROTREKL (1920)
Poet
Brno

Ivan Klíma

SOCIETAL EVIL
AND TOLERANCE

Tolerance is one of those values that appears at first sight to be exclusively positive – such as, for instance, truth, peace, humaneness or freedom. But of all these concepts, tolerance, I would say, is the most relative. Or as Bochenski put it, when understood as an absolute rule, tolerance is a superstition.

Recently I read in an English-language anthology an excerpt from a novel by an Albanian author. It tells the story of a scientist, a member of the Albanian minority in Kosovo, who dreams of one day overcoming the thousand-year-old hatred between Serbs and Albanians. He dreams of an Albanian Romeo and a Serbian Juliet achieving understanding and celebrating their marriage in love and peace. But just when it seems that love actually has a chance to triumph, national unrest erupts, tanks shoot into crowds, and his Romeo is one of the severely wounded.

The belief that appeasement can overcome societal evil is an illusion, and quite a dangerous one, as we have seen so many times in our century, especially those of us born in the center of Europe. It was thanks to appeasement that Hitler was able to begin his preparations for the biggest war in history and that Stalinism swelled to such monstrous proportions.

Many times I have asked myself why people repeat the same mistake over and over, looking on passively as something ruinous runs amok around them. Apparently the problem is not whether or not people want to be tolerant of societal evil, but whether or not they manage to recognize it in time.

With the passage of time, now that we know the consequences of the ideas, conceptions and intentions of this evil, it tends to seem less ambiguous to us than it did to its contemporaries. But the fact is that opinions as to what is good or bad for society or for human beings vary according to time, location, tradition,

culture, religion and hierarchy of values; moreover, they are often subjected to irresponsible manipulation.

But let's return to the story of the Albanian author. It is prose
written à la thèse, but what fascinated me was that even though
it was written prior to the war now raging in the former Yugoslavia it posed a critical question: Can one dream of love and tolerance in the face of intolerant nationalist fanaticism?

Also I was intrigued by the problem of how this question
could be formulated in a work of literature. The author sought to
demonstrate the perniciousness of nationalist hatred, and yet
he was so biased in favor of one side that he only reinforced a
dualist view of the world in which one group personifies evil and
violence, the other good and reconciliation. In the end, this only
supports the way of thinking that is clearly guiding the behavior
of the people in this region: They're hitting us, so we have no
choice but to hit them back!

Almost no one today could doubt that it was tolerance of Hitler's racial and nationalist theories that cleared the way for the
hysterical violence that followed, despite that at one time a significant number of Germans, including German intellectuals,
believed that Hitler's teaching would help them in the struggle
against evil – personified for them not just by Jews, not just by
the Weimar democracy, but also by most of the countries that
defeated them in World War I and forced their generals to sign
a treaty that was generally considered to be humiliating.

The "death sentence" handed down by the Ayatollah Khomei-
ni on Salman Rushdie was for nearly everyone who subscribes to
our culture a case of virtually inconceivable fanatical intolerance; for many Muslims, however, it was an exemplary condemnation of a societal evil that sought to debase the Law they acknowledge.

In the history of Judeo-Christian culture, too, including the
Bible, one of its cornerstones, we could find judgments whose
severity would be inconceivable to us today. Not to mention
those grandiose visions of a classless society in which hatred
was to disappear along with crime and all other nastiness, in
which the arts and sciences were to flourish like never before in
history. It is almost unbelievable how many great minds suc-

cumbed to this illusion and how fanatically they thundered against anyone and everyone who refused to share their illusion.

Heretics, Jews, women stamped as witches, opponents of geocentric theory, atheists, believers, opponents of monarchy, supporters of monarchy, capitalists, opponents of capitalism, socialists, opponents of socialism – every one of these was at one time or another considered a societal evil that had to be eliminated.

Unfortunately literature – and I do not mean by this the substandard pamphlets of ideologues – has all too often served to unleash the dangerous demons that slumber within human nature instead of helping to keep them safely tucked away.

It was the renowned realist literature of the last century, guided by its compassion for the oppressed and the impoverished, by its feeling of responsibility for the world of human beings, that first saw (and depicted) society chiefly as the setting for injustice, current events as a breach of the established order, and the world as a battleground, where some become rich at the expense of others, where the happiness of the few is secured by the haplessness, even the suffering, of the many.

Societal evil for the realists was increasingly personified by those representing wealth, capital, enterprise and the petty bourgeois mentality (all caricatured, of course, as covetous, squandering and greedy), while the destitute (les misérables), the wretched and the exploited increasingly enjoyed their sympathies, or at least their compassion.

While these writers depicted only the fates of individuals, all the ideologues needed to do was take that one small step and generalize from those fates, using them to bolster their racial or class theories.

At the beginning of our century, the artistic avant-garde considered the petty bourgeoisie the most contemptible form of life. For them the petty bourgeoisie were not only narrow-minded and limited, but even worse, orderly, clinging to tradition, with a lack of imagination and therefore no understanding for progress and experimentation, for new ideas and artistic trends.

These avant-garde artists were the ones who took that logical step, renouncing contemporary society and welcoming the vision of a newly ordered world, a more just society that would not only eliminate the differences between the rich and the poor (take from the rich and give to the poor), but also wipe out the loathsome petty bourgeoisie and educate a new audience who would properly understand the revolutionary meaning of avant-garde art. Thus, in the name of an illusion about the future, these artists became the messengers of intolerance in the present and did so with a clean conscience.

Obviously what I have in mind here is not the degenerate literature of ideology, justifying police violence and glorifying intolerance, informing, spy-mania or outright dictatorships. Most of these writers did not celebrate either intolerance or the most barbarous form of violence that comes from it. Nearly all of them rejected World War I, and wars in general, as excessively violent and senseless, as well as lacking in any sort of lofty aims. But revolution was something entirely different.

In many cases those who were considered the great minds of the era welcomed revolution, and for many years and decades they were willing not only to condone but even to defend the violence of revolutions, which, as they saw it, served a purpose – after all, revolution stamped out a societal evil they had been pointing out for decades and opened the gates to the illusory world of their dreams. This was just as true of Robespierre's revolution as it was of Lenin's.

A significant portion of world literature was at least tolerant if not actually supportive of the ideas that served as the basis for the bloodiest regime of this century, while their attitude towards its victims ranged from blindness or apathy to intransigence.

Our century is a century of intolerance. Hatred was the cornerstone of its two prominent ideologies. Two devastating wars turned the human world of values upside down. The Christian faith in the power of atonement on the one hand and forgiveness on the other was shaken to the very core. In this part of the world, the aftermath of this sudden dislocation of values was a totalitarian society that outlasted the lives of two generations – more than three in the case of the Soviet Union – during which time it did its best to make this dislocation into the prevailing canon of human behavior.

The chaos, the violence, the fratricidal hostilities, the calls for revenge, the flaming passions that have afflicted our part of the world since the fall of that system, founded on the teaching of hatred as the driving force of society, could only surprise those who ignored the ruinousness of what came before.

To resist emotions in a situation like this is not easy. Many writers even feel it is their obligation to voice, to articulate with precision these emotions and sentiments. I, however, feel a different obligation.

We are entangled, it seems to me, in a chain of guilt and shared guilt (for to be silent was also to share in the guilt) both for the crimes of the past and for the retribution taken for those crimes. Retribution, however, usually leads only to further crimes and injustices, which in turn require further retribution.

I feel the obligation to search for a way to break this chain. For me as a writer that means taking an interest in the fate of humans, in characters, situations and chance encounters in which this chain either breaks or crumbles.

In 1969, my colleague Jiří Stránský, who spent more than eight years in Communist concentration camps, published a book of stories called *Štěstí (Happiness)*. This book was unique among those that dealt with life in the camps, for it searched out the moments of happiness amid the horror. Most of the time the source of this happiness was some chance encounter or even the fact that the others, the guards, were capable of acting in a humane way. Stránský's was a book that spoke of the worst that can happen, and yet it managed to break that chain I am speaking of.

I have never overestimated the importance of literature or its influence on the fate of the world. I am convinced, nonetheless, that we writers have one great privilege, and as a result, one great responsibility that goes along with it: We create our own world. For this world, for this world alone, we bear complete and supreme responsibility; not, as some writers so proudly and mistakenly persuade themselves, for the real world. Whether we authors like it or not, however, it is this world of ours that readers compare to, if not identify with, the real world.

I am convinced that an author jeopardizes his or her work, and above all the authenticity of his or her world, the moment he or she attempts to drag into it the oversimplified ideas, emotions and intolerance that reign in the real world.

"Ordinarily, people have precious little room to set aside in the world of values; whenever there is room for one, another one must be pushed aside," the Czech writer Karel Čapek lamented more than fifty years ago. "As a result of this furious evaluation, we live in a horribly devalued world; from this springs the catastrophic mood seizing people today; it seems to us that there is no use regretting a world in which there are so many things we renounce with indignation."

It is my impression that in the fictive world of today, in which the writer alone reigns supreme, violence, anger and crime are on the rise; scheming is repaid with scheming, betrayal with betrayal, or at least infidelity. By this I do not mean to claim that writers are taking the side of the world of decay. On the contrary, they often write about these phenomena because they condemn them.

I recall some years ago, when I finished reading Heller's *Something Happened*, a most provocative novel, it occurred to me that with his pathos, his indignation at a life lacking in any sort of higher aspiration, he reminded me of the Old Testament prophets, who censured and denounced the Israelites for their sins. But unlike the prophets, who offered order to the people in the name of the Lord, he evokes in those who listen to him nothing more than feelings of desperation, disillusionment and depression. And it is these feelings that eventually give rise to the revolts which we are witnessing today and whose consequences are unforeseeable.

I don't believe you could find a single important work of literature calling for intolerance or for violence outright. But you could find many more works – written often out of good will, naiveté, or sheer calculation on the part of the author – that generate in people a feeling of dissatisfaction, of contempt for the fate of ordinary people, of disgust with the world. And often these same works create the illusion that there exists some other possible human world, some better world, and that it is necessary for some to bash others in order to attain it. Literature such as this may generate intolerance where, in fact, there is a much greater need for understanding, modesty, patience, forgiveness and constructive efforts.

Obviously the limits of tolerance and intolerance in literature cannot be set from outside; no measures or definitions can be found. Only thoughtfulness and responsibility on the part of those who write can determine the limits.

As Karel Čapek once said, the writer must realize that his or her work "will not be the instrument of any intellectual one-sidedness, that it will serve nothing but intellectual integrity, nothing but the totality of man."

IVAN KLÍMA (1931)
Novelist and dramatist
Prague

Josef Škvorecký

THE BETRAYAL OF COMRADES

*An excerpt from
the novella NEUILLY*

But first, how political schooling can hypnotize. A dangerous thing if you're young, undamaged, if you still feel that the most important thing is to JOIN FORCES WITH OTHERS to change the world and eradicate all the evil (when the truth is that anything you can do has to be done as an individual, alone, and only within the range of your immediate environs or, if you're really lucky, within the range of your readership, and then, you can't really change the world, at best you can improve it, and even so, good people will improve, and bad ones don't read fine literature). Dangerous indeed.

I was young, already primed by Benno (if Benno does, son of a rich man, why not me, son of a white-collar worker?), and there, facing us at the political schooling lecture at the lovely little hotel stood a magical hypnotist with the hands of a laborer and a canny eloquence. What was fantastic about him (and hypnotic, too) in those days of prefabricated, modular clichés, was that he spoke in his own words. He had a gift for translating hackneyed phrases into ordinary language, in fact, into the local Eastern Bohemian idiom, the gift of a writer, the essence of writing. There I was, young, primed by Benno, with the scruples of bourgeois kids, their social conscience overstimulated by Reverend Fathers, and I listened to that articulate ex-laborer, and that ex-laborer explained, "It's not a matter of gossip. It's a matter of comradely, collective help. If we want to help – and we truly do, we want to help everyone, indiscriminately – we have to know, and understand. Everyone has different faces that he shows to different people, without even realizing it. We need to know all those faces, and by projecting them simultaneously onto a single screen, we can assemble every comrade's genuine, inner countenance. We'll recognize what troubles him, where his uncertainties lie, and we'll help." I felt a mighty yearning for help, everything troubled me, and despite having been primed by the ingenuous Benno, I was certain of nothing. "I'll pass around some questionnaires," said the ex-laborer, "one for each of your fellow teachers at the school. And you'll take them and fill them out, anonymously, of course, so as not to make you feel hampered by any (absolutely groundless) fear that the comrade might find out what you have written, and you'll put down, without reservations, the pure and complete truth, as you perceive it. That's the only way you can help." I took the forms he distributed, and, primed and hypnotized, wanting to help and wanting to be helped, I penned horrible truths, item by item, without reservations.

The faculty at the school where I taught, probably a typical one, consisted of a group of committedly intractable non-Marxists. Of course, for the most part everyone was a member of the Party; perhaps the only ones who weren't were the music teacher and me. Teachers are the avant-garde; they are all supposed to be in the Party and their livelihoods depend on it. Yet I was amazed by their astonishing immunity to science, in particular to the Science of all sciences. To them, it was all asinine: the exploitation of the working class, the privation of the proletariat, surplus value, to each according to his need, socialism, absolutely everything. I couldn't understand it. Today, I do, I see that it was only this irrational immunity that saved us, that under (the new) broad-scale humanism, (the old) small-scale humanism had not quite died out. Perhaps. But at the time, the flames of idealism were licking at my heels. I wasn't burning yet, just beginning to kindle: Málek, Josef, schoolteacher, I wrote. And I proceeded to mete out item after item. "A comrade without the foggiest notion of what it's all about." Yes, I doled it out: "He still believes in God, no, in a god. He tells political jokes." Criminal hypnosis. Under that muddling of minds – perhaps they had put something in the hotel coffee, too – I turned into an abominable Morozov, a phantasmagoric monster. Hypnotized as I was by the canny anti-Fascist with a working-man's hands and the gift of language, if they had come to me and handed me an application to join the Party, I would have signed up.

Fortunately, Comrade Canny made a mistake. He distributed
the questionnaires before lunch, to be filled out over the break,
and as I sat on a bench in front of the hotel, dispensing incriminating truths, all of them absolutely truthful and all of them –
though I didn't realize it at the time – grounds for dismissal,
grounds indeed for arrest and imprisonment, all of a sudden, as
the hypnotic voice in my head began to fade, the hypnosis began
to dwindle too, the way alcohol (maybe there really was something in the coffee) evaporates, my writing slowed down, the
worm of alcohol-induced (drug-induced, mass-suggested) certainty gradually spun itself into a cocoon, and the head that
poked out of the cocoon was that of the beautiful butterfly, prin-
cess Uncertainty. She sneezed in the sunlight, and I was overcome with the writerly need to stop for a while, to read something. A comrade happened to be walking past with several copies of the latest *Rudé Právo*; he gave me one, I opened it, and –
that instant of all instants, perhaps all that is left of religion: at
a moment of elemental crisis or the bleakest of desperation,
something happens that looks for all the world like coincidence,
someone calls, a sentence on a page of a randomly opened book
catches your eye and deflects the crisis, a letter arrives, something happens, an absurd God working in an absurd way, *credo
quia ridiculum* – my eye fell on the headline in *Rudé Právo*:
SUBVERSIVE GROUP SENTENCED. Members of the Boy
Scout movement. And they doled it out, the way I had to my
colleagues (Josef Málek taught singing, and singing was probably the only quality thing taught at that awful school): Jarmila
Ebenová, born 1932 (my moment of Temptation, even more dangerous than the Temptation of St. Aloisius, by the plump bosom
of an unchaste phantasm), 15 years in prison; Jiří Kořínek, born
1933, 20 years; Dagmar Želivská, born 1932, 10 years. The year
was 1950, before I heard about the unmarked graves; the curtain had yet to rise on the bizarre vaudeville that was to be the
Slánský trial. But certain events that had happened earlier, in
Kostelec, events I barely registered back then, in my youthful
diffidence, they began to take shape through the fog of the imposed ideology: Ruda Mach, arrested as an army officer, sentenced to 18 years. Benda's benign face by the swimming pool

called Jericho: "Soon as I was behind bars, first thing, I got busted in the snoot!" which cast some light on that science, that willingness to help; it was as if I had suddenly leaped out of a mud
bath and stood there naked, muddy, surrounded by people with
their clothes on. In fact, I actually shivered.

I picked up the form bearing my unfinished help to comrades
(help for sure, comrades indeed, but which ones, which comrades?) and left in the direction of a room that is significant in
all dictatorships, i.e. the toilet, where you get rid of love letters
that could land you in the clink, and foreign currency and address books, because if they were to find anything like that on
you during a search, say, at the border, they could turn you
around and send you back, even though your trip is paid for in
full and you have every possible clearance (what treasure troves
the toilets in border-town taverns must be for the science of
snooping; maybe they've even come up with a machine for sal-
vaging soaked and flushed notebooks). I locked myself in there,
surrounding myself with the last bit of privacy left in dictatorships (not even that, though; my friend Kathryn once discovered
a little microphone under the rim of the toilet bowl in her room
at the Hotel Kiev in Moscow – an example of the concrete music
of the KGB, the only modernistic music in the USSR). I took out
some matches and set fire to my perfidious effort to help the
comrades, because my formative years spent under dictatorships aroused in me a gnawing uncertainty. I wasn't even sure
whether the Teachings, the science of sciences, hadn't come up
with a method whereby even torn-up shreds of urine-soaked
paper could be extracted, recombined, smoothed and deci-
phered, thus ensuring that despite the best efforts of a paper-
tearing, urinating reactionary spoiler of their helpful intentions,
the comrades WOULD be helped, willy-nilly. So I burned the
papers to ashes, and after I had stirred up the ashes in the toilet
bowl with the rolled up *Rudé Právo*, I pulled down my trousers
and shat on it all, using the dry part of *Rudé Právo* to wipe
myself (naturally, there was no toilet paper, which isn't an anti-
quated joke but a bare-assed reality). Then I flushed it all down
the drain, which fortunately wasn't plugged up the way it usually was.

Having undergone this ritual of purification, I returned to the empty classroom, picked up a clean set of questionnaires and proceeded to fill them with personal observations about my colleagues that glowed with the uniform countenance of Exemplary Comrade with Positive Outlook. I lied like a rug, and the comrades could take it all and stick it where the sun don't shine. As the Reverend Father Meloun once declared, taking pen in hand to forge an entry in the Parish Record about a marriage between an Aryan lad and a Jewish bride: "Under certain circumstances, an act of deception can turn into an act of Christian charity." I had deceived the comrades, the worse comrade I. I was sure that all my colleagues had described one another the same way, with a Positive Outlook, but then, of course, I could easily be wrong. Not everyone would have happened onto the *Rudé Právo* in the nick of time. Who knows. Who knows.

JOSEF ŠKVORECKÝ (1924)
Novelist and essayist
Toronto

Jiří Stránský

GOOD BLOODY FRIDAY

(Part XIII from the collection
"On the Far Side of the Fence")

On the day that you are hog-tied and dying of thirst
somewhere on the banks of a torrent
and they thrust a kerchief
wet with pepper water
into your mouth
attempt in your mind at least
to wish for that mighty one
who might have avenged you
to forgive
the hand that put the kerchief
into your mouth.
Just try!

JIŘÍ STRÁNSKÝ (1931)
Novelist
Prague

Karel
Šiktanc
NIGHTFALL

Stink of roses
silence at the very brink of tears

from the barbershops in the darkness
the eternal glory snip-snips away
and Sleeve Pond smooths out its creases and folds...

what less? with rag hands
we hang onto our settees on our becurtained floor
so our heads are not struck off from below

Someone struck a match:
blanched white elephantiasic hands – scrubbed
joints polished humps and veins –
suddenly brighten a little bit above the ground and stirringly
dance in air with a snake-skin scintillation
inside the mischievous haze
like the fatal center of the world!

the domain of the moment
quivers with sacred stage fright thunders without heart
in the fingers with penetrating screeches
on the outskirts of villages open the gates of the senses

the spirit of God freezes in fear
ceramic gutters clink through the thirsty garden
a night insect sculls and the great beings of loves
and parents...
a tree like an unhearkened tale

Fall where they say
basely beheaded

The Castle Emptiness hollers
the dramatic starkly pallid body of lust coruscates
and a child shies away red as a lamp before the wan
hard face of the moon
frozen in fear God's wraith the Word God's wrath
through the bus station trots a dog bearing
a beslobbered stick

Are we all here?

cash register rings
knickers on a line – stripped misfortune

blindfolded I embrace the first living thing
frantically I clasp it, the very first to be
strangled
only so it groans only so it cries out
so it's not struck by the thought of being dead

KAREL ŠIKTANC (1928)
Poet
Prague

Milan Uhde
SYMPOSIUM
ON TOLERANCE

In the depths of the Sixties, when forbidden and forgotten topics were beginning to return to writings and conversations on Czech soil, the admirers of a poet were sitting around him in a wine bar, urging him to share his views on tolerance.

Instead of giving them an answer, he told them how one day, as a country schoolboy, he had made up his mind to test the tolerance of his catechism teacher.

He waited until after class and said: "Reverend, sir, I've been thinking a lot lately about the Virgin Mary's Immaculate Conception."

The catechist looked the boy up and down haughtily, and in three words conveyed his superiority, as if the questioner were not thirteen, but seven or five. The words: "Go fuck yourself."

The poet took a lengthy drink of his red wine. But it was not a pause; it was the end of the story.

His listeners' faces filled with bewilderment. What did the poet mean by that? That country priests are pigs?

One of the men at the table, a sworn atheist, said it out loud: pigs and primitives. But the poet would neither confirm nor deny his view.

Could he have meant his story to prove something so banal? No, I would wager that the catechism teacher spoke neither more nor less candidly than anyone else in his community when they were rejecting someone or something.

Then someone at the table voiced the enlightened idea that a doubting thirteen-year-old should be treated democratically and with decency. It is the religion teacher's duty, he said, to hear the boy out, to discuss his doubts and to instill in him a sense of respect for Mary as a courageous woman and mother.

In the end, nearly the entire auditorium was in agreement that the teacher had been intolerant. In those days, people like that were called dogmatic, meaning that instead of thinking, they merely repeated precepts received from others.

Seated around the table were scholars of the Old and New Testaments, as well as of the history of the Inquisition and of the classics of both the theory and practice of violent revolution, and they put in their two cents, saying that the advocates of intolerant attitudes were dangerous because they were capable of killing, even mass murder, in the interest of their teachings.

The poet went on sipping his wine in silence.

I tried to bring to mind the scene he had described. I could see the thirteen-year-old framing his question, and it seemed to me I could feel what it contained.

It was more than merely an intellectual questioning of the miracle, the sort that can strike thoughtful people at a tender age – an attitude which later, with experience, either changes into certainty or else blows over; because miracles are either a fiction, or on the contrary, a reality. No, in my opinion, the thirteen-year-old felt an urge to provoke his teacher, to manhandle something that was sacred to him, to broach a subject that was not open to discussion. The teacher's reply, therefore, was absolutely appropriate.

Those who sing the praises of tolerance like to stress that educated Europeans have won for themselves the right to pose any question to anyone. The problem is that they can expect tolerant answers only if the questions are posed in a tolerant way.

But the poet's tale has yet another dimension. For the country priest plays the role of both administrator of truth and teacher of mystery, a position which is fragile and problematic. It will always be put to the test and cast into doubt. This is the lot of those who play that role. The wise among them know this.

Administrator of truth, teacher of mystery, defender of order: contradictions not only for the instincts of a thirteen-year-old, but especially for the adult examiner. The administrator of truth is at the same time its confiner, for truth cannot be administrated; the teacher of mystery is its simplifier, for mystery cannot be instructed; the defender of order is a jailer, for order cannot be imposed; thus spoke the most esteemed guest at the poet's table, the philosopher and champion of human rights. His words exuded the truth of merciless reason.

They begged the poet to pronounce a straightforward verdict, but he remained silent for the rest of the evening. For he knew the inscription at the old Jewish cemetery: "I have grown wiser with the years. What is wisdom, I do not know."

The philosopher presided over the discussion, testing those present (and especially those absent) in tolerance, and handing out grades. He reminded me of a thirteen-year-old schoolboy prodding his catechism teacher.

No one recalled that teacher's three words. But they hovered over the table like stirred-up old dust.

MILAN UHDE (1936)
Dramatist
Brno

Contents

Contents – – – 237

LIST OF TRANSLATORS
Anna Bryson (AB)
Louis Charbonneau (LC)
Jana Klepetářová (JK)
Randall Lyman (RL)
Noreh Hronková (NH)
Káča Poláčková-Henley (KP-H)
Iris Urwin (IU)
Paul Wilson (PW)
Alex Zucker (AZ)